YOUR STORY'S NOT OVER

JIM KING

Published by Insight International, Inc.
contact@freshword.com
www.freshword.com
918-493-1718

ISBN: 978-1-960452-15-3
E-Book ISBN: 978-1-960452-16-0

Library of Congress Control Number: 2025906170

Printed in the United States of America.

DEDICATION

IF A STORY IS supposed to have a hero, mine is named Pam, my wife. She consistently amazes me. Our journey has had some interesting twists, and she has been more than up to the challenge for them all, and by my side every step of the way. I love you, Pam, more than ever. Stay like you are. There may be more stories ahead.

Our two children, Drew and Natalie, had front-row seats to many of these stories. Always without complaining about having to give up some of the comforts of life, they willingly embraced God's plan for them in His story. I could not be more proud of you both. I am grateful God gave you great spouses in Stacy and Eric. You still amaze me as I watch you raise the six most beautiful, amazing grandchildren in the world: Ella, Winston, Korbin, Josephine, Kaiden, and Malcolm. (PLI)

CONTENTS

Acknowledgments

AT A CASUAL BREAKFAST a number of years ago, a friend of mine encouraged me to write a book about the stories I had seen God write. He even told me how to do it. He is definitely qualified to tell one how, as he is one of the most prolific writers in America. Thank you for the encouragement, Bob Burke.

I knew I needed help. John Mason, founder of Insight International, has been the key to bringing this to life. Without you, John, it would not have happened. It has been a joy to work with you on this. Thank you for your patience with me. I cherish your friendship.

Kim Spence was on our second crusade team in Stavropol, Russia, in early 1993. Not only have her writing skills brought life to this project, but she is also part of the story. Thank you for your excellence, Kim. I am so glad you were on that trip over thirty years ago.

INTRODUCTION

THIS IS A BOOK of stories. Some from Bible times, and some contemporary. There is one common denominator—they all give honor to the greatest storywriter of all time. God has been writing beautiful stories from the beginning of time. Just look around at His beautiful creation.

I'm not a storywriter, but God is. I can only tell a story as He wrote it. However, none of us would have a story worth telling without Him.

If you choose to go on this book journey with me, please keep in mind the personal stories are not about me and Pam. They're about Him. We are simply characters in the storyline. So are you. Yes, your story is different than ours, and it is supposed to be. The Master storywriter has a different story to tell through all of our lives. No one among us has a story that is more important than another, but we each have a story to tell.

Some of you are in the middle of a life story that has you questioning how it will turn out. My prayer is that somehow God will inspire fresh hope within you and strengthen your faith to believe that God is about to write a beautiful new chapter in the story of your life. To encourage yourself, look back, and reflect on how God came through in one of the past storylines of your life. Then, look forward knowing, Your Story's Not Over!

CHAPTER 1

WHISPERS ON THE LIVING ROOM FLOOR

IT WAS DECEMBER 1991 in Tulsa, Oklahoma. At that point, Pam and I had spent thirteen years in an itinerant ministry. I had preached across America and one country overseas, Brazil. I enjoyed it, but I had no more passion for preaching overseas than I felt for preaching in America.

We were in a season of, *"Lord, what are you saying? What are you doing? Where are we going?"* Perhaps you have been there.

On that December day, for whatever reason, I felt a prompting to fast until dinnertime. Nothing in particular was going on. I intended to fast and spend more time in prayer. I knew the house would be empty in the afternoon, so I went home. As I lay on my living room floor, I heard the voice of the Lord, perhaps more clearly than ever before. It was so impacting that I could show you where I was lying and how I was sprawled out on the floor. I wasn't praying for anything specifically other than the Lord's direction in our lives.

Then, I heard the voice of the Lord! *"I have called you to go around the world."* It was so loud and clear in my spirit, it almost seemed as if it was an audible voice. It was not audible, but it was solid and clear. I heard words that I would not have thought of, which is one reason I knew it was Him and not me.

We all have pivotal moments in our lives—when the details seem permanently etched in our minds. Ladies, you can tell me a specific outfit you wore when you met your future husband, or men, you probably remember the smell of her perfume on that first date.

If I ask you where you were on 9/11/2001, you'd be able to recall the exact spot when you first heard about the horrific attack on America. You could probably remember the weight of disbelief as you watched the tragedy unfold.

Those life-changing moments stay with us.

What about when you surrendered your life to Jesus Christ? Do you recall that moment? Maybe you were in a Sunday morning service and felt the tug of the Holy Spirit calling you. Or perhaps you were in an old-fashioned tent revival, or maybe you were by yourself out in the wilderness, and you knew God was real, and you called out to Him at that moment.

Those are pivotal moments when you know beyond a doubt that God has spoken to you. I'm talking about where the Holy Spirit takes hold of your entire being to get your attention for a moment so crystal clear that you will never forget the room, the smell, the sight, the people, and the moment God changed everything in your life.

That was my experience that day in December 1991, and God's timing is incredible!

ANSWERING THE WHISPER

Only about a month after that experience, in January 1992, I received a phone call from Miriam Machovec. Miriam assisted Bob Hoskins and his son, Rob Hoskins. Bob is the founder of an organization named OneHope.

Perestroika (restructuring of the Soviet Union's economic and political systems) had just occurred. The walls were coming down, and people were gaining access to the country. OneHope was the first organization invited by the Russian government to put Bibles in schools in a vast land that had denied its citizens access to the Gospel for seventy years. What an opportunity!

OneHope founder, Bob Hoskins, took quick action. Bob and Rob soon saw the opportunity to conduct evangelistic crusades in the evenings after American teams had conducted assemblies in the schools during the day.

They were formulating their strategy at that time, and someone recommended they call me to see if I wanted to speak at one of those crusades. So, that's how I received the call soon after I heard the Lord say, *"I have called you to go around the world."*

Miriam said, *"You've been recommended to us. Would you be willing to speak at a crusade in Russia?"* I said, *"Where do you want me to go?"* She said, *"Irkutsk, Siberia,"* to which I half-jokingly replied, *"I'll get back to you on that."* Siberia wasn't on my bucket list.

For those of you who are like I was then, having no idea where Irkutsk is on a map, if you were to take a globe and put a knife through it from the point where I was living in Tulsa, OK, you would pierce the globe on the other side of the world at almost exactly Irkutsk, Siberia.

When I looked at that, I remembered the words, *"I have called you to go around the world."* You can't get any more "around the world" than that. So, I felt I had my direction and was supposed to go. In April 1992, I met a small group that OneHope had assembled in Moscow. From there, we took another all-night flight to Irkutsk, Siberia. I was "around the world." That week was one of the most memorable and meaningful ones of my life.

Some of you will remember the images displayed on American television during those days in the early 1990s, images of people across Russia standing in lines waiting for bread. It was a nation broken by the extreme socialistic system, leaving massive numbers of people jobless and hungry. Unfortunately, that was not their greatest need; they had been left with a spiritual void. A deep chasm of hopelessness fueled the churches, having been destroyed and driven underground, resulting in seventy years without the Light of the Gospel.

When I came home from Irkutsk, my wife, Pam, asked, *"What was it like?"* I said, *"If I could have gotten you and the kids there, I never would've come home, because I saw such abject hopelessness on the faces of people like I've never seen before."*

Soon after I spent that week in Irkutsk, Siberia, OneHope called me and asked, *"Would you be willing to go again?"* I said, *"Yes."* It's amazing how God will give you a heart for people worldwide, even after just one trip. I knew I would want to return. They said, *"We want you to go to Stavropol, Russia."* I said, *"I'll go."* In early spring 1993, I returned to Russia.

Thankfully, Stavropol was not in Siberia. It is located between the Black and Caspian Seas, between Europe and Asia. During the trip, when the various groups of our ministry team went to schools and different places around the city, I often went with them.

On our first day there, I took a small group to a kindergarten to do an assembly and distribute Bibles (the *Book of Hope*). I introduced them and sat down by a window. Looking out the window, the Lord spoke again clearly, like in December 1991.

I heard these words, **"Kyiv, live here."** These three words would dramatically change the course of our lives. But looking back, the chain of events began at the moment of my surrender when the Lord said, **"I have called you to go around the world."** If I hadn't surrendered my heart to that calling, I might have missed it when He called us to Kyiv.

Courage Beyond Comfort

Many times, the Lord will give you somewhat of a big picture, just like He did with Abraham: *"He took him outside and said, 'Look up at the sky and count the stars—if indeed you can count them.' Then he said to him, 'So shall your offspring be'"* (Genesis 15:5), and *"I will surely bless you and make your descendants as numerous as the stars in the sky and as the sand on the seashore. Your descendants will take possession of the cities of their enemies"* (Genesis 22:17).

God did not tell Abraham all the details at that point in time. He gave the big picture and filled in the pieces of it as Abraham went along. God often reveals His plans to us the way He did to Abraham—step by step, piece by piece. He gives us the big picture and the promise but leaves the details to unfold in His perfect timing. This isn't to overwhelm us but to grow our faith and trust in Him. If He showed us everything all at once, we might focus too much on the challenges rather than the journey. By guiding us one step at a time, He teaches us to rely on Him daily, to walk with Him closely, and to discover His grace in every moment. It's in the unfolding that we see His hand at work, shaping us into who He created us to be. The journey is as much about transformation as it is about the destination.

As I sat with the weight of God's call to move to Kyiv, I couldn't help but wonder—*"How is it going to happen?"* The details were unclear, and the path ahead felt like uncharted territory. All I had was the certainty of His voice and the promise He had spoken. I didn't have answers, but I knew the One who did. This was the beginning of a journey that would require faith in every step, trusting God to open doors, provide resources, and make a way where none seemed possible. He had shown me the destination, but the process of getting there would be revealed in His time. Looking back, I see that God wasn't just calling me to move to Kyiv but to trust Him in a way I never had before. The "how" wasn't my responsibility; it was His. My responsibility was to say yes.

CHAPTER 2

TAKE THE CALL

YOU LIKELY THINK THOSE three words that changed everything were *"Kyiv, live here."* But I could also add three more words: *"Take the call!"*

When you need to talk to your spouse about something during the day, and you call, but it goes to a voicemail like, *"This is Pam. I'm sorry I can't take your call right now. Leave a message,"* you know the feeling you get—all you can think of at that moment is to say, *"Take the call!"*

I regularly receive calls on my mobile phone from numbers I don't recognize. Most of us do. I do not answer those calls but wait to see if they leave a message and identify themselves. Sometimes, I take the call if I recognize the area code and think it might be someone I know. Sometimes, I am wrong; it is a telemarketer. There are times I missed it—I should not have taken the call. And yes, there are times I am glad I took the call, like the one that came to me in January 1992 from OneHope.

I received that call, and it changed Pam's and my life. But that call was not the one that changed our hearts. It was the call that set the course. That call would never have happened if I had not answered another call long before that.

Please indulge me for a moment, because I must share a little background so you can truly understand the good part of this story and what this book is about.

I was privileged to be raised by wonderful parents in a Christ-loving, God-honoring home. My family has a long history of serving the Lord. My great-great-grandmother on my dad's side started an Assembly of God church in her living room in 1924. Today, it is a vibrant church called SpiritCHURCH that is located in my hometown of Bartlesville, OK. My mother's side of the family also goes back generations in faithfully serving the Lord. I am grateful for that heritage. Although that is important, *taking the call* is a personal decision.

I had a conversion experience between the eighth and ninth grades when I genuinely surrendered my life to Jesus' lordship. I can take you to the spot; I know where I was. After that, I had a love for God. I wasn't perfect, but I was a teenager who tried to serve the Lord and wanted what He wanted. However, I wasn't on a mission to go into the ministry. It's the last thing I ever wanted to do.

All I wanted to do was play sports. But that dream came to an end when I suffered a very severe knee injury in high school. After graduating, I needed guidance about what to do, so at seventeen I enrolled in a junior college in Miami, OK. Through a series of events during the second semester of my freshman year, I got involved in the leadership of a campus ministry group called Chi Alpha. One nondescript evening, our Chi Alpha group gathered on campus to pray together. There was no speaker or worship team. It wasn't a service; it was just college students meeting to pray together. It was during that prayer time that I heard the call clearly.

Wrestling with the Call

God's plan for my life was to preach the Gospel. So, I ran! No, not toward God, but the other way. I am not proud of it, but I did everything possible to escape it for about four months. I could not picture myself standing in front of people speaking. It petrified me, as I was very shy in that regard.

You might wonder, *"How did you know that was the call that night?"* I wish I could tell you in simple form. But if you receive a call like that, you know! It was the deepest of impressions inside me, an inner knowing without doubt. One thing is certain—it didn't come from me because it would have been the last thing I desired.

I tried making a deal with God, telling Him all the good things I would spend my life doing. Perhaps I could be a dentist who can help people by pulling their aching teeth. Or a fireman who can rescue people from blazes. But to no avail. The call would not go away! That's the thing about a call from God in a person's life; it will not go away. Romans 11:29 says, *"For the gifts and the calling of God are irrevocable"* (ESV). Another Bible translation says that they are *"never canceled, never rescinded"* (MSG).

Finally, I surrendered and enrolled in Central Bible College (now merged with Evangel University). However, I still resisted the call I knew God had placed on my life to preach the Gospel. So, I had only partially surrendered. I decided to go to where He chose to help me develop the call, but I had not fully submitted to do what He said for me to do. Therefore, my first semester at Bible College was miserable.

I remember the cold February night that first year of Bible College, alone in my dormitory room, falling across my bed and telling God, *"Yes, I will preach."* But I said, *"Don't ask me to travel. I won't do that."* What's that old saying? Something like, "A man makes his plans, and God laughs." Here's the thing about *the call.* It is pretty much nonnegotiable.

Unconditional surrender to the call is required for the call to come to fruition. So, I spent a few more miserable weeks and finally told God, *"I don't know how, when, or where, but I surrender to the call You have placed on my life and trust You with it."*

When you stop running from the call, you should start running toward the call. All the time we spent avoiding doing what God has asked should now be spent doing everything possible to fulfill His mandate in our lives. I will spare you most of the details, but I started doing things to prepare myself for whatever the call would involve. I began admitting to the necessary people in my life that I was called to preach and that I had surrendered to the call. I told my roommate, friends, and pastor—people who would hold me accountable. When the opportunity came calling that summer after my first year of Bible College, I preached my first sermon at Oglesby Assembly of God in Oglesby, OK. I am not sure you'd call it a sermon, but I gave it a shot. Pastor Paul Stetts was brave enough to submit his congregation to my efforts to pursue the call. I will always be grateful to him.

If you are called to preach—or whatever He has called you to—it is a great comfort to know that the Master Teacher, Jesus, said, *"I am with you always, even unto the end of the world"* (Matthew 28:20 ASV). Whatever the call on your life, He is with you.

When it was time for me to answer the call regarding a move around the world, it was one thing to commit a week or two to go to Russia and conduct a crusade, knowing I would quickly return to the good ole USA and my wife and two children. But the idea of uprooting and moving my family to a place I had barely heard of was a different story.

I knew nothing about Kyiv except that it was the capital of Ukraine, and the name of a chicken dish people cooked called Chicken Kyiv. I probably couldn't have found it on a map, but I had heard those words, *"Kyiv, live here."* In three words, God defined everything. The place of assignment was Kyiv. The length of the assignment was not clear then, but it was simply, *"Live there."* I wouldn't have lived there without the three most important people to me: Pam, Drew, and Natalie.

Even when you get a word from God, remember that His timing is vital. He wants us to agree with and cooperate with Him. And when we do, there's power released . . . in our marriage, in our church, in our business, in every aspect of our lives. When we are aligned with God, His power is released into the situation. At the heart of the issue is that I want what God wants with my life because He wants better than I want for my life.

Although I've heard God speak to me and can mark many of those distinct moments in my life, as mentioned before, this would forever change the trajectory of my family.

After the experience in the school in Stavropol, even though I knew the Lord had spoken to me distinctly about going to Ukraine and moving my family there, I didn't want to. It was that simple. Later, I will tell another part of the story that was so convincing. But for now, suffice it to say, I knew I was to move our family to Kyiv.

On the flight home from Stavropol at thirty-five thousand feet up, I recall looking out the airplane window at the blue sky with the sparkling Atlantic Ocean below and saying to the Lord, *"How do I tell her [Pam] this one?"* It was a valid question, don't you think? I heard the Lord gently whisper, *"Plant a seed."* In other words, don't be a dummy by walking through the door and saying, *"Hey baby, guess where we're moving?"* He meant, just drop a hint and let Him do the work. It would take time because, up to that point, Pam had not personally experienced what I had.

That idea of not dumping the whole story on her at once is good for any marriage. Genesis 33 records Jacob's return with his family when he went back to his homeland after a twenty-year hiatus due to having to flee for his life from his brother Esau. It was a journey of perhaps a few hundred miles over arduous territory with livestock and small children. Genesis 33:14 says, *"I will lead on gently"* (ASV). That's what the Lord was trying to show me. Sometimes, once I have reconciled something in my mind, I can charge ahead without considering the effect on others. Again, there were and are no others more important to me than Pam, Drew, and Natalie. Family before ministry!

I knew my wife would go if she were convinced that I had heard from the Lord. And Pam is sensitive to God's voice. On my own I was willing to go anywhere or do anything, but moving her and our two minor children was a different ball game.

Earlier I mentioned that my family has a one-hundred-plus-year relationship with the Assemblies of God and that I felt God's call to ministry during my first year of college. I received ministry credentials soon after, and in the summer following my *"Kyiv, live here"* experience, I heard that the Oklahoma Assemblies of God was having a five-day summer meeting series, called a camp meeting, in Oklahoma City. I had to go.

I don't know who spoke or what he spoke about, but I can take you to where I stood at the front after the speaker had opened the altar for people to pray. I was there trying to get out of going to Ukraine. I heard the voice of the Lord as clear as a bell saying to me, *"If you do this, I'll bless you."* I wasn't looking for a blessing. I was trying to get out of it.

What I could see ahead was a path of great difficulty. How would I get the money to do this? How would I even get there? How will our children handle it? Scripture tells us in Proverbs 3:5-6, *"Trust in the Lord with all your heart, and lean not on your own understanding; in all your ways acknowledge Him, and He shall direct your paths"* (NKJV). Trusting His reasoning over ours is hard for most. Yet, it shouldn't be, because we know He knows much more than we do.

But I had to make up my mind at some point. Finally, after much internal wrestling, I told the Lord, *"I'm all in. I'm submitted to You. You're my Lord, You're my Master, You're not just my Savior."* Our relationship with God is not an insurance policy. It's a relationship. I told Him, *"You are my Lord. And I'm going to go."*

You have to get beyond what you see naturally. Spiritually, almost everything that happens has a corresponding action attached to it. You must take the call when it's Jesus on the line. We all have a calling, a purpose for being. For some, it is spending your life in full-time ministry. But for a majority of us, it is fulfilling your purpose in the marketplace.

Sometimes that requires us to change our thinking. The most extraordinary ministry often doesn't happen behind the pulpit; it occurs in the marketplace. And we can all relate to knowing that many people are in need. So, if He does place a call, it might be for full-time ministry, but more likely, He's calling you to join a team in your church to serve where you are. Everyone's call is unique to them. No one's call is more important than any other person's on earth. It's all about the one person who can reach another person for Christ.

FULLY SURRENDERED, FULLY SENT

One of the biggest challenges in missions is staying focused on what God called you to do and what He spoke to you to do. You will encounter so many things that need to be done. There are so many good causes. The anointing is not being in a cause that is just a good cause. The anointing is being in the cause that God says is the cause for you—the difference between a good idea and a God idea.

When we received the call from the Lord to move to Ukraine, I knew it would be the most significant change of our lives up to that point. But even after moving in the summer of 1994, we had to stay open to hearing the Lord for other changes that would be made along the way. We couldn't get stuck on the one-time call. I constantly had to be willing to let the Holy Spirit lead me into areas that required me to change or for me to change something.

Later in the book, I'll share stories of how God sometimes prompted us to change course, even going into the Middle East. If I had not been willing to change, I could have stuck my heels in the ground and said, *"God told me to go to Ukraine. I'm staying in Ukraine. I'm not going anywhere else. I'm staying right here."* I could have stayed there and been partially obedient to God. However, I learned something vital: Partial obedience is disobedience.

In the spring of 1995, God began to speak to me about shipping humanitarian aid into Ukraine. I didn't want to do it. I didn't like the idea. I said, *"I'm not a doctor, I'm not a nurse, I'm a preacher."* As if God cared. God could see that this would be the key to keeping the door open so we could preach the Gospel. More on His purpose is discussed later in Chapter 7. His plan is always best, and so are His ways. We just simply had to change our method. We didn't change our principles, and we didn't change our message. The message never changes.

There might be different methods of getting the message out there, and what do we care, as long as it's the most effective? If God said, *"I'm going to start moving through bagpipe playing,"* I'd get a bagpipe, put on a kilt, and learn how to blow that thing . . . simply because God says that's how He wants to do it.

We have to be willing to be pliable. I found that as long as I stay pliable before the Lord and say, *"God, not my program, not my little idea, not my little plan, God, not what I want, but what You want,"* that's when God is able to do the most. If you want what God wants in the days ahead, you must accept the fact that the future never looks like the past. Never.

Recently I was reading an article about stupid quotes, which were stupid things that people have said. One of them was that the head of the US Patent Office in 1895 authored a bill in Congress that stated they should close down the US Patent Office. He said all the great inventions ever to be discovered had already been discovered. In 1895. Wouldn't that guy die again if he could come back to life and see everything that's been invented in the last one hundred years? He'd flip out when he saw a cell phone or when an airplane flew over his head, wouldn't he?

There are many things you have to accept by faith when it comes to embracing change. I don't know how black cows eat green grass and give white milk and yellow butter; I just know they do. So, when I've got butter on the table, I'm not going to try to figure it out; I just taste it, and I know it's good.

When God begins to impress change, when God begins to speak change, and when God by the Spirit begins to orchestrate change, it is ALWAYS for the advancement, the betterment, and the good of His people. God is not against you. God is for you. God is always looking out to do good and not harm. Evil doesn't come from God. Evil comes from the devil, and good comes from God.

Though our flesh may resist it, we've got to recognize that if God said to change it, then there must be something good God has in mind. I'm going to be better off than I was before. God is taking us forward, not backward. He's taking us up, not down. We're going ahead, and we're not going backward. That's why change has to come.

The Bible says, *"Eye has not seen, nor ear heard, nor have entered into the heart of man the things which God has prepared for those who love Him"* (1 Corinthians 2:9 NKJV). I don't know everything God wants to do. I just know I take it one step at a time.

Proverbs 23:7 says as a man *"thinks in his heart, so is he"* (NKJV). You're either going to think big or small, victory or defeat, good or bad. So, if you're going to think, why don't you just go ahead and think big? Let's think bigger than we're thinking right now. Let's begin to think beyond what we see right now. Let's begin to think that God could do exceedingly abundantly above all we ask or think according to His power that works in us. Let's begin to think about entire communities being touched by the Gospel of Jesus Christ. Let's think outside the little framework that we have grown up within.

What is significant and popular today isn't what was important and popular twenty-five years ago. That's the way it ought to be in the church world. That's the way it ought to be in the kingdom of God. What was big then is not big now. God is not shrinking. God is not downsizing. God is not selling off. God wants the thing to get bigger and bigger and bigger. He's not willing for anyone to perish but for all to be part of His kingdom.

Some people have a poverty mentality and think that we should just scrape by, scrimp by. Think beyond that. Think bigger than what you have experienced. The Bible says that death and life are in the power of the tongue, and those who love it will eat its fruit; as a man thinks in his heart, so is he; out of the abundance of your heart, your mouth will speak. Change your thinking, and it will change your speaking.

When it came time for me to step out and accept what God said about changing and moving, there had to be action that demonstrated faith and trust. *Trust is the link between hearing God and obeying God.* In the Bible, Jesus told the man with a withered hand, *"Stretch forth thine hand"* (Mark 3:5 KJV). To the man who had lain on the mat for decades, Jesus said, *"Take up your bed and walk"* (John 5:8 NKJV). They were required to show that they trusted Him by putting action to the words Jesus spoke.

The Lord had been trying to show me. There at that altar of that camp meeting in Oklahoma City, I saw problems, and God was trying to get me to see that He had already begun releasing His blessings in remarkable ways.

It would take some miracles . . .

CHAPTER 3

WAITING FOR RAIN: TRUSTING IN DRY SEASONS

DREW, OUR FIRST CHILD, was born in 1980, and it should have been a season of celebration and joy. But just a few months later, in the middle of our new family's bliss, Pam's father passed away unexpectedly. He was only fifty-five years old at the time, leaving my mother-in-law a widow at forty-six. The grief that followed was like a shadow that loomed over us. Pam was especially devastated, and it seemed like everything came crashing down all at once. She was flooded with her own grief, as well as trying to manage her mom's grief combined with exhaustion from caring for a newborn and the challenges of life in ministry.

But the difficulties didn't stop there. Soon after her father's passing, Pam started getting ill. At first it seemed like something that the emotional stress and fatigue of recent events could explain. But as time went on, it became clear that something was very wrong. She experienced sharp, cyclical pain that would come in waves, hitting her hard every thirty days like clockwork. Every month, without fail, she would become violently ill, unable to keep anything on her stomach for up to ten days at a time.

We went to doctor after doctor, trying to find answers. They all had their theories: stress from her father's death, postpartum complications, hormone imbalances, and maybe some mental issues. But none of their treatments worked. They prescribed medications, ran tests, and even hospitalized her multiple times, yet Pam continued to get worse. We couldn't find a specific answer from any of the experts except that her blood work was out of whack. All this time, we were still traveling in ministry. Pam would be in extreme pain, yet when it was time for her to sing at a church service, something miraculous would happen. The moment she stood on the platform and began praising God, the pain would vanish—only to return once the service ended.

I vividly remember one particular occurrence. Pam was in so much pain that she could barely stand. My mother-in-law had prayed every prayer she knew, and nothing seemed to change. Then, she started singing. As long as Mom kept singing, Pam's pain would fade. It became our refuge—worship was the only space where Pam could find relief. It was quite an emotional roller coaster.

Four long years of suffering passed before we received any real answers. During this time our daughter Natalie was born in December 1983. Desperate for a solution, we decided to go to the City of Faith hospital in Tulsa. There we met Dr. Don King, a man of faith and a skilled physician. He examined Pam, ran more tests, and finally, he came back with a diagnosis: Familial Mediterranean Fever, which is a rare, inherited, incurable autoinflammatory disease. While we were relieved to know what was causing her sickness, the words *"no cure"* hung heavy in the air. Dr. King reassured us with something far more important: *"There is no cure,"* he said, *"but we know the Healer."*

God had given Oral Roberts a dream to build the City of Faith so that patients would come to it, God would work through medicine and prayer, and people would be healed. We chose that place with the idea that God would provide answers through whatever means possible. We were strong in faith that Pam would receive her healing, and we were willing to go anywhere and do anything to stand fast and believe God for it to happen.

Because we heard that some of Oral Roberts' family visited the hospital at times, we asked the nurses if any of the Roberts family might be coming over to pray with patients at the hospital. They told us that occasionally they did, but only occasionally.

One day, they were going to run some tests and do a biopsy, and because it had been so painful previously, it made Pam incredibly anxious to think about another one, so they gave her a sedative. She wasn't knocked out, just relaxed. About that time, I went into the hallway near the nurses' station and saw Oral Roberts walking down the hallway. The nurse told me he was coming in to see Pam.

Excitedly, I walked back into the room and said, *"Pam, he's out there and coming to your room! Oral is coming to your room!"* Well, I have to confess something here: I'm known to be a bit of a jokester at times, so my wife thought that announcement was anything but funny as she replied, *"Be quiet and leave me alone. I just want to sleep."* I told her I wasn't teasing, and at about that time, one of the nurses rushed in to confirm the news. Pam said, *"Oh my goodness, give me a brush, and at least let me brush my hair!"*

And in walked Oral Roberts.

THE PROMISE IN THE PAIN

He didn't offer a long prayer or any grand gestures. He simply told Pam to repeat after him, *"In the name of Jesus, I am being healed."* The room was thick with God's presence as she spoke those words—it felt like electricity. We both wept as Oral hugged us. He turned to start walking out the door, but turned back and said, *"That's what He told me to tell you."* And he walked out.

One of the strangest things happened; she was dismissed shortly after that, and when we went home, she had one of the most horrific bouts of sickness ever. The war was on.

But the day after that visit, something changed in our spirits. We knew deep inside that healing was on the way. We left the hospital with that hope in our hearts. We didn't know how or when, but we believed God would heal Pam. We held on to every scripture verse we could find on healing, confessing the Word daily, sometimes multiple times a day. We prayed and believed, even when it seemed like nothing was happening.

One day, Pam was lying on the couch, exhausted from yet another round of illness, when the doorbell rang. A woman named Lenora, someone Pam had met at a Bible study, was standing at the door. Lenora had never visited us before, and Pam was in no condition to have company, but something told me to let her in. She walked into our home and said, *"The Lord gave me this verse for you, Pam."* She opened her Bible and read Exodus 23:25: *"He will bless your bread and your water. And I will take sickness away from the midst of you"* (NKJV).

It was a simple verse we had read many times before, but it was like a light switched on at that moment. The words came alive. Immediately, I knew we had to act on this. I went to the pantry, grabbed a can of chicken noodle soup, and warmed it up. Pam hadn't been able to keep anything in her stomach in days, but stepping out in faith, I asked her to sit up and eat. *"The Word of God says you're healed,"* I told her, referring to the verse Lenora had just spoken. *"Try this."*

She did it. Every bite stayed down, and from that day forward, she was healed. It didn't happen overnight because there were a few short-lived battles. There was still a fight of faith, but we knew that God had touched her body. Pam never missed another service after that. She wasn't just enduring anymore; she was walking in her healing.

TRUSTING DURING THE WAIT

As I reflect on Pam's healing journey, I can't help but think of Noah's story. His life is a timeless example of what it means to hear God, trust Him, and obey Him, even when the situation seems impossible.

A friend of ours once said, "Freedom is not the absence of something. It's the presence of Someone with you in the middle of the situation to walk you through it successfully."

Imagine being Noah. God tells him to build an ark—not near a lake or ocean, but in the middle of dry land. The very idea was absurd, yet Noah didn't waver. He heard God's voice and trusted that what God said would come to pass, even if it made no sense at the time. Hebrews

11:7 says, *"By faith, Noah built a ship in the middle of dry land. He was warned about something he couldn't see and acted on what he was told"* (MSG).

Noah's obedience was immediate, even though the results of that obedience wouldn't be seen for many years. He built the ark while people likely ridiculed him, questioning his sanity. But Noah trusted that God's word would be fulfilled in due time. Then finally, the Bible says the heavens opened, and for forty days, it rained in a straight downpour.

Even then, the journey wasn't over. After the rain, they were stuck in the ark for over a year. Think about that—a year of living in a floating zoo with your in-laws and all those animals. The manure alone would test anyone's patience. Yet, Noah trusted God's timing. He didn't rush to get out when it seemed like the rain had stopped. He waited.

Why did they have to stay in the ark so long? That's where trust comes in. Noah had the word from God. He had the experience of hearing directly from the Lord, which carried him through the waiting. Noah's obedience required steadfast trust and patience. Trust doesn't always lead to instant results, but it does lead to God's perfect timing.

Noah didn't just hear God's command to build the ark; he trusted that what God said was coming actually would, and that trust compelled him to act in obedience. Obedience isn't always easy, and it often requires stepping out in faith before we see any tangible evidence.

One of the most amazing acts in the Bible is that Noah built that ship over a span of about 120 years. He remained faithful to the cause God gave Him based on one word that came to pass 120 years later. Most would have given up. If you find yourself laboring in an assignment you know the Lord gave, stay with it. Don't quit. Some people live their lives looking for the next "word" when they haven't completed the last assignment He gave. God's reward is sure for those who remain true to His assignment and calling, even when it is tough. Obedience is often not easy.

After he finally got in the ark, Noah spent over a year there, waiting for God's next move, just as we spent four years waiting and believing for Pam's healing. But the wait is always worth it when God is the One leading the way.

Genesis 8:13 tells us that the ground's surface was dry, but God saw beyond the surface. He knew the earth wasn't ready to sustain life yet, so He instructed Noah to remain in the ark a little longer. Noah probably didn't understand, because the surface of the ground looked dry from his vantage point inside the ark. It wasn't until nearly two months later that God finally told them to leave the ark.

How often do we find ourselves in a similar position? We look at our circumstances and think, *"This looks fine. I can move forward,"* but God says, *"Wait."* His timing is perfect, and sometimes the wait is God's way of protecting us from things we cannot see. Noah's wait was not a denial of God's promise but a protection from the destruction that still lingered outside the ark.

I think about that when I reflect on my own family, especially when God called us to move to Ukraine. When God speaks to you directly, pushing through the hard times is easier because you know what He said. But that doesn't mean it's easy for everyone else, especially those who weren't part of that initial experience. Pam is one of the strongest women I know—she will have ten more crowns than I'll ever think of having—but even for her, this was a massive leap of faith.

When God first spoke to me about moving our family to Ukraine, it was clear and undeniable. But it wasn't something we had ever dreamed of, and it was a big ask. We all know how mamas are, and Pam is no different—she's a mama bear—taking her kids halfway around the world to a place that wasn't exactly stable at the time required serious trust.

I had to know that I knew this was from God. And Pam had to trust not just God but me. That's no small thing, especially for a wife who has to follow her husband into unknown territory. Noah's daughters-in-law didn't hear the word from God firsthand, but they got in the ark anyway because they trusted Noah. It's the same dynamic. Pam didn't hear the call to Ukraine directly, but she trusted that I had, and that was enough. When a husband leads a family in faith, the responsibility is heavy. There's no room for inconsistency or doubt.

Looking back, I'm grateful that Pam had known me long enough to trust that I wasn't someone who changed my mind every six months. That kind of inconsistency breeds insecurity in a marriage. Early on, when we were dating, I had a clear sense of my calling. I struggled with accepting it at first, but once I did, I knew I was meant for an itinerant ministry. That conviction laid the foundation for our relationship, and Pam saw that. She knew I wasn't going to change my mind about what God had called us to do, even if the specifics—like Ukraine—came much later.

When the time came to bring up Ukraine, I didn't rush her. I planted the seed. I knew God had to work in her heart like He had worked in mine. And over time, He did. She began to feel the same stirring that I had felt. Pam started asking questions like, *"Where were you when God spoke to you about this? What were you wearing?"* She needed to know the details, and I could tell her because when God speaks, those moments are etched into your mind forever.

It was a process. Pam had to trust that if God had called me, He had also called our children. God reassured me during one of my prayer times: *"My will for you is My will for them."* Our children are His first, and He's as concerned about their path as He is about ours. That's when Pam and I knew—this was a family calling, not just a personal one.

When God says it's time, that's when you move. Not a minute earlier, not a minute later.

Reflecting on Noah's story and our own, I've learned that trust is not passive. It's active. Trust means waiting when God says wait and moving when God says move. It's holding on to His word, even when the results don't come as quickly as we'd like. It's leading your family with confidence, knowing that if God has called you, He will provide the way. It's understanding that His timing is always perfect, and when the opportunity of a lifetime comes, you must be ready to act.

Many of us know an old song "'Tis So Sweet to Trust in Jesus." It was written by a lady named Louisa Stead on the heels of one of her life's darkest moments. She and her husband had one young daughter named Lily. They lived in New York on Long Island. One day, the three of them went out for a picnic. While relaxing, they heard a boy scream for help from the water, and they ran to the shore. As Louisa and Lily stood on the shore, Mr. Stead jumped in to try and save the boy. As they watched, before their very eyes, Mr. Stead and the boy both drowned. This plunged them into practically complete abject poverty because Mr. Stead was the family breadwinner.

One day, Louisa sat down and began to write the words for the song "'Tis So Sweet to Trust in Jesus."

"'Tis So Sweet to Trust in Jesus" by Louisa M. R. Stead (public domain)

'Tis so sweet to trust in Jesus,
Just to take Him at His Word.
Just to rest upon His promise.
Just to know, "Thus saith the Lord."

Refrain:
Jesus, Jesus, how I trust Him!
How I've proved Him o'er and o'er!
Jesus, Jesus, precious Jesus!
O for grace to trust Him more!

O how sweet to trust in Jesus,
Just to trust His cleansing blood.
Just in simple faith to plunge me
'Neath the healing, cleansing flood!

Yes, 'tis sweet to trust in Jesus,
Just from sin and self to cease.
Just from Jesus simply taking
Life and rest, and joy and peace.

I'm so glad I learned to trust Thee,
Precious Jesus, Savior, Friend;
And I know that Thou art with me,
Wilt be with me to the end.

The Lord sustained Louisa and Lily as they walked through this dark valley, and it was not the end of their story. Eventually, they became missionaries to South Africa. God redeemed their situation for His purposes. But I must admit that, sometimes, trusting in Jesus doesn't feel so sweet. Sometimes it's not so easy, but He's worthy of our trust because He sees the end from the beginning. Only He has the solution to every problem we face.

Pam and I decided to follow God's leading to Ukraine, one of our most significant acts of trust and obedience. It wasn't easy, but we knew that if God had called us, He would be faithful to complete the work He started. We heard Him, we trusted Him, and we obeyed Him. And He has never let us down.

We knew it was time to go because the opportunity of a lifetime must be seized during the lifetime of an opportunity.

CHAPTER 4

FEAR'S WHISPER, FAITH'S ROAR

FEAR AND TRUST ARE two forces in life that are in constant opposition. Fear often creeps in when we are about to step into new, unfamiliar territories. On the other hand, trust calls us to take the leap, believing that what's on the other side is for our good. It's counterintuitive, but true childlike faith is about living in that place of trust, where fear does not have the final say. Again, the opportunity of a lifetime must be seized during the lifetime of an opportunity. That means if you're going to fully trust God, you must conquer fear and step out on whatever opportunity God puts in front of you because sometimes the opportunity fades.

Think back to one of the most well-known moments in history: the Israelites at the Red Sea. After escaping Egyptian bondage, they stood on the shores of an impossibility—water ahead, the Egyptian army behind. Fear gripped them. The temptation to go back to slavery must have been overwhelming in the face of certain death. But God showed them that His timing is always perfect. At just the right moment, He parted the waters, made a way where there was no way, and took care of their enemies in a spectacular fashion. This was a moment where faith was tested, but God showed His faithfulness.

Exodus 14 says the people cried out to Moses. He replied, *"Do not be afraid. Stand still, and see the salvation of the Lord, which He will accomplish for you today. . . . The Lord will fight for you"* (vv. 13-14 NKJV). God parted the Red Sea, and the Israelites walked across on dry ground. One problem . . . here came the chariots right after them. Man cannot outrun a chariot. I love what God did. *"The Lord looked down upon the army of the Egyptians . . . and **He took off their chariot wheels**"* (vv. 24-25 NKJV).

FACING THE GIANTS OF FEAR

How often do we face situations where the circumstances seem insurmountable? When fear tells us to give up, childlike faith tells us to keep trusting, even when we can't see the way forward. God's timing is perfect, and often His answer comes in the "nick of time." That's why we must seize the opportunities He presents us with complete trust in His wisdom and timing.

I want to share a family story that shows the importance of never giving up, even when fear and doubt seem overwhelming. My father, an only child, had two cousins—Bernard, who became a preacher, and Charles. Charles was a good, hardworking man, but I had never seen him show much interest in God. My dad loved Charles like a brother, and he tried to talk to him about his faith throughout his life. But every time Dad brought up God, Charles would tune him out.

Charles had a godly mother, my Aunt Art, who prayed fervently for him. In her nineties, she lost her sight but still lived alone in her home. In her last years, before she had to go into a skilled nursing facility, she lived with Charles.

So here you have this praying mama who loved God with all her heart, mind, soul, and strength and raised her two boys the same. One son, Bernard, followed the path of serving God and was in the ministry; the other, Charles, chose a different path. Although Charles never wanted to talk about God, he truly loved his mama. She was smart like a fox and never preached to him about God. Instead, she loved him.

When Aunt Art moved in with Charles in her later years, she insisted that every Sunday morning, he read her the Sunday school lesson from her church despite his reluctance to talk about God. Because of his love for his mother, he would do it. The Word of God slowly began to sink into his heart, even though he didn't realize it. She lived to be 105, and she used to say, *"I call the name of every person in our family in prayer every day before the Lord."*

For years, it seemed like nothing would change. Then, Charles suffered a major heart attack. My dad and I visited Charles in the hospital. Dad asked, *"Charles, have you ever made it right with God?"* And in his cold, seemingly unfeeling and unemotional tone, he said, *"No."* And my dad asked, *"Are you ready to right now?"* And seemingly cold again, Charles answered, *"Yes."* We paused for a moment. To our amazement, Charles not only said yes, but he also wept his way to Jesus. Charles is in heaven today with his praying mother.

Why did it take so long? Only God knows. But this story reminds us that we can't give up, even when it seems like nothing is happening. God works in His time, and our part is to trust Him, even when we can't see the outcome. Fear of disappointment, failure, and rejection must be conquered if we are going to live a life of trust.

Those are the same areas we all face, whether talking to a relative who seems so far away from God or if we're in Ukraine trying to figure out where to live.

We get frustrated with God's timing but forget that He sees what we can't. Imagine how impatient Noah and his family must have felt. But God's timing was perfect. Remember, even when the ground appeared dry, God knew it wasn't ready to sustain them. Had they stepped out too early, they would have faced disaster. Sometimes, the wait is God's protection. He sees the bigger picture, and we have to trust that He knows best.

That's why trusting God's timing is so crucial. We may be ready to act, but if He says to wait, we must believe there is a reason. Fear often makes us want to rush ahead, but trust tells us to wait for His perfect timing.

Here's an excellent example of God's perfect timing regarding my wife, Pam, and me. Pam and I go way back, further than most people realize. We've known each other since I was eleven years old and she was ten years old. At that time, her father became the pastor of our church. We went to the same schools and shared many of the same friends. In high school, we started dating.

We had what you might call a typical high school relationship—full of ups and downs, young love, and dreams for the future. At that time, neither of us had any idea what God had in store for our lives. After high school, our paths separated for a while. Pam went off to Oklahoma State University, while I answered the call to ministry and went to Bible College. We were both on different tracks and, at one point, didn't date each other at all for about eighteen months.

Looking back now, I realize that God had His hand on our relationship from the very beginning. Even during our time apart, He worked on both of us, preparing us for the future He had planned. When we reconnected, it wasn't just a reunion of old high school sweethearts—it was a realization that our lives were meant to be intertwined for something far greater—His purpose.

By the time we got back together, I was sure of two things: first, that God had called me into ministry, and second, that Pam was the woman He had chosen to walk that path with me. Pam loved God but had her own dreams and ambitions. The idea of a life in ministry didn't exactly line up with the future she had envisioned.

Had we married straight out of high school, the story would probably be a lot different today. God used that time we were apart in our early days of college to form His plan individually in each of our hearts. Time was needed, and time apart was needed. With God, timing is essential. It was a season in which we began to fully trust that God had a perfect plan for our lives. Although we could not see the fullness of His plan, we both found a place of submission to Him.

Pam came to accept that God's call on my life was also a call on hers. We weren't just partners in life—we were partners in ministry. We've always had a strong foundation of trust in each other, which I believe comes from knowing each other for so long. But more importantly, we learned to trust God together. When we finally got married, we were aligned in our purpose and ready to serve the Lord, no matter where He took us.

FACING THE UNKNOWN TOGETHER

That foundation of trust would prove to be essential later when God called us to leave everything familiar and move our family to Ukraine. Pam wasn't hesitant because she lacked faith; she just needed to be sure. After all, she wasn't just being asked to support me in ministry—she was being asked to take our children to a foreign land with all the uncertainty that came with it. But our long history together, both as a couple and as believers, gave us the strength to face the unknown.

God has a plan not only for individuals but also for families. When God called us to Ukraine, Pam was concerned about taking our kids to such an unstable region. But God reassured me that His will for me was also His will for our children. Trusting that God's plan for our family was good helped us to move forward as a unit despite the fear of the unknown.

Let me back up here and tell you about Pam's moment to take that leap of faith and overcome her fears. I had been traveling to Ukraine and Russia for ministry trips for a while, but Pam had never gone with me. She always said she would go one day but had concerns about leaving the kids. Her biggest worry was finding someone to watch them while we were both away.

One day, seemingly out of the blue, my mom called Pam and offered to come and stay with the kids while we went to Ukraine. It wasn't like my mom to offer something like that, and Pam knew this was a God-ordained moment. There were no more excuses. Pam agreed to come with me, and that trip would change our lives forever.

During the trip, Pam saw firsthand the work that God was doing in Ukraine. God spoke to her heart, confirming this was where we were meant to be as a family. The opportunity to serve there was undeniable, and God had been working on both of us to step into that calling together. Once Pam overcame the initial fear, she could see how God's hand was guiding us. Remember earlier, though, I mentioned that God told me to plant a seed for Pam. When we listen to God's instructions and trust His timing, we will get God's results.

When I first felt the call to move our family to Ukraine, I knew that the biggest hurdle wasn't logistics—it was convincing Pam. She had supported my ministry, but asking her to take our children to a foreign country, especially one as volatile as Ukraine at the time, was another level of trust altogether. I knew my wife.

Pam had a deep faith in the Lord and would do anything He asked, but taking our babies into such an unpredictable situation would require more than just my reassurance.

I remember praying and saying, *"God, if this is Your will for us, You are going to have to convince Pam, because I can't."* It wasn't enough for me to feel called; she had to hear it for herself. She needed to know with certainty that this wasn't just another ministry trip but a life-altering decision for our whole family.

Pam asked all the tough questions: *"Where will we live? How will we keep the children safe? What does God want from us there?"* She wasn't against the idea, but I knew that deep down, her concern was for our children. She once told me, *"I'll go wherever God wants, but I need to know this is His will for Drew and Natalie, too."*

God, in His faithfulness, answered those prayers. It bears repeating that one day He spoke to my heart as clearly as ever: *"My will for you is My will for them."* That was the confirmation I needed. These weren't just my children—they were His children first. I had to trust that what God was asking of me, He was also asking of them. Pam, too, came to the place where she knew in her spirit that this move wasn't just for me but for our whole family. Once she felt that assurance, she was ready to make the leap of faith.

WALKING ON THE UNSEEN PATH

Pam insisted that if we were going to live there, we needed a three-bedroom apartment—one room for us and one for each of the kids, partly because the kids would be homeschooled and need their own rooms. Finding a three-bedroom apartment in Kyiv was like finding a needle in a haystack, but Pam was determined. The Soviets did not build many three-bedroom apartments. It would be a rare find.

In the summer of 1994, I went to Ukraine to speak at a conference and look for an apartment. I found a place that seemed perfect—three bedrooms, two bathrooms, and in a nice area of the city. It was everything we needed, and I was ready to sign the lease on the spot. But as we pulled up in front of the building, I felt a strong, inner voice telling me to wait.

I went inside to look at the apartment, and everything seemed great, but I couldn't shake that feeling of unease. It was like God was saying, *"Not this one."* I knew I had to listen, even though it made no sense. I told the agent, *"I can't sign this. I don't know why, but I feel like I'm supposed to wait."*

Walking away from that apartment wasn't easy. It felt like the right fit on the surface, but I had to trust that God knew better than I did. The challenge with waiting was that I was returning to America the next day and moving my family to live in Kyiv the very next month—without a place to live. The three-bedroom apartment I turned down was the only one we had found.

We were moving in August, and my parents had decided to fly over with us and stay two weeks and help us get set up in an apartment— which we didn't have. Since they were coming with Pam, Drew, and Natalie, we decided I should go three days before them, hoping and praying that I could find a place. Two days before they arrived, a friend called and said, *"I found another three-bedroom apartment."* We quickly scheduled an appointment. It was spacious with large rooms and three bedrooms and was half the price of the other one. I learned it pays to listen when it doesn't make sense.

This apartment was in a Ukrainian neighborhood where we could live among the people and not be isolated as foreigners. The building was filled with everyday Ukrainian families, and that's exactly where God wanted us.

At first the neighbors were suspicious of us—foreigners coming in and hauling lots of equipment. The older women, known as *babushkas*, would sit outside watching us every day, giving us disapproving looks.

Pam eventually joked that they probably thought we were part of the mafia, with all the things we were loading in and out. We kept all our PA equipment for our crusades on our enclosed balcony. But over time, things softened as our children started playing with the local kids. Our daughter, Natalie, picked up Russian quickly and began explaining to the other children what we were doing. Evidently, word quickly spread throughout the apartment building. Soon, the *babushkas* waved and smiled, welcoming us into the community. It was a small miracle, one we never saw coming when we were struggling to find the right place to call home.

We later realized that this apartment, in this particular neighborhood, allowed us to build relationships and be part of the community in a way we couldn't have imagined. God's timing and placement were perfect, and it reminded us that sometimes, when He says to wait, He has something better in store that we can't yet see. And as I said, half the price.

Opportunities often come at the most unexpected times. They may not look like what we envisioned, but if we trust God, we must be ready to seize them when they come. Fear will tell us to wait, analyze, and second-guess, but faith tells us to move forward when God opens the door. Again, the opportunity of a lifetime must be seized during the lifetime of the opportunity.

We can take comfort in knowing that God sees what we can't. He orchestrates every detail, and when the time is right, He will bring the right people, resources, and opportunities into our lives. We must be willing to step out in faith, even when fear tells us to hold back.

Ministering in Your Sphere of Influence

One of the things I've come to realize over the years is that ministry isn't just for the preacher standing behind the pulpit on Sunday morning. We often think that serving God means you must be in "full-time ministry" or be a pastor, but the truth is that God has called each of us to serve Him in whatever sphere of life we find ourselves. Whether you're a teacher, a businessperson, or a stay-at-home parent, your work matters to God. You have a place in what He's doing.

The Bible teaches us that the body of Christ is made up of many parts, and each part is essential. It says in 1 Corinthians 12:12, *"For as the body is one and has many members, but all the members of that one body, being many, are one body, so also is Christ"* (NKJV). You may not be called to preach, but that doesn't mean your role is less valuable in the kingdom of God.

I've met people who work in all kinds of fields—business owners, doctors, insurance agents—who often feel like their contribution to God's work is less significant because they're not in traditional ministry roles. But nothing could be further from the truth. The Word of God wasn't written for pastors alone but for all of us. It's meant to guide every aspect of our lives, including our work.

I believe that many people in the business world, education, government, and other professions are positioned by God to have a tremendous impact on the kingdom. Some of the most influential people I know aren't preachers—they're business leaders who take God's love into their workplace every day. They interact with more people in their field than a pastor might on any given day, and their influence stretches far beyond the walls of a church building.

Our first convert when we moved to Ukraine was named Victor. In the crusades, we saw large numbers of people come to faith in Christ. Victor was not one of them. Earlier I mentioned that when we moved to Kyiv, my parents traveled with us and stayed for two weeks. I hired Victor as a handyman to install cabinets in our apartment. During the day, I would be out and about in the city. Dad stayed at the apartment so our wives would not be there alone with a stranger. Victor spoke a little broken English. One day, my dad realized he had a Gospel tract in his coat pocket. It had been there for weeks. He wasn't sure Victor could even read it, but he gave it to him. Victor immediately sat down on the couch and read it. Dad said it took a while. Victor's English was not very good. When he finished, he looked at Dad and said, *"Mr. Frank, I believe every word of this."* Dad replied, *"If you do, do you want to pray that prayer with me?"* They knelt beside the couch in our living room, and Victor surrendered his life to Christ. He and his wife Halina still serve the Lord faithfully today.

I often remind people that the father of faith, Abraham, wasn't a preacher. He was a businessman, a shepherd, and a leader in his community. But God's promises to him weren't based on his profession but on his faith. And just like Abraham, we all have a role in God's plan, no matter our profession. Whether you are leading a business, working in an office, or serving at home, your faith can influence those around you.

I've seen it time and time again: When people live out their faith in their everyday lives—by running their businesses with integrity, treating their employees and customers with love and respect, or even just by being a godly example to their coworkers—God's work is being done. That's ministry.

Your calling is just as important to God as any pastor's. You are valuable in His kingdom, and your work—whatever it is—matters. More than the world needs more preachers, it needs more believers who will live out their faith in whatever role God has placed them. God has uniquely equipped each of us to bring His love into the world through the work He's called us to do. So, never underestimate your role in the kingdom. Whether you're sitting at a desk or standing on a stage, you're serving the same God, and your contribution is part of the bigger picture of what He is doing in the world.

This understanding—that ministry is not confined to the pulpit but is lived out in every part of life—became even more real to us once we moved to Ukraine. When we arrived in Kyiv, we knew that God had called us there for a reason far more significant than we could have imagined. Just like in business or any other field, when God calls you to do something, He equips you for it. He doesn't just plant a dream in your heart and leave you to figure it out alone. No, if God puts something in your heart, He will put it in your hand.

That's precisely what we experienced in Kyiv. We didn't have all the answers, and we certainly didn't have all the resources when we arrived. In fact, there were many moments of uncertainty, moments where fear could have quickly taken over. But God had already put the vision in our hearts, and we trusted He would provide the means to see it through.

Whether you're running a business or answering a call to ministry, the principle is the same: God gives us what we need when we need it. His provision comes when we step out in faith, trusting that He will guide us, just as He did for us in Ukraine. We didn't know then that our work in Kyiv would extend far beyond the crusades. We couldn't have predicted the doors that would open or the miracles we would witness.

But we were about to experience firsthand that when God calls you to step out, He will also equip you for the journey ahead.

Faith, after all, is stepping out on nothing and landing on something . . .

CHAPTER 5

STEPPING OUT ON NOTHING AND LANDING ON SOMETHING

FAITH OFTEN FEELS LIKE stepping into a void, into nothingness, and hoping for a solid foundation beneath your feet. It's the story of so many biblical heroes and even contemporary ones. When we say, *"Faith is stepping out on nothing and landing on something,"* we are talking about acting on belief, often without any guarantee of what comes next. It is acting because you know, deep down in your spirit, that God is faithful.

It's the kind of faith Pam and I had to live by when we were called in Ukraine to establish an orphanage called House of Joy. I want you to see that faith doesn't always start with a burning bush moment; it grows incrementally. Each step builds upon the last as God proves Himself over and over again.

The Call to Ukraine: Stepping Out Without Knowing

In 2004, I was contacted by the director of education in Kakhovka, Ukraine. She asked Pam and me if we would help them establish an orphanage. Like so many others, this city was struggling with the aftermath of political unrest and economic hardship. Children were living on the streets, and there wasn't a place for them. The city had this dilapidated seventeen-year-old building—gigantic, abandoned, and in desperate need of renovation. The government offered it to us but with no funding. They couldn't officially give us the building, but we could take it and renovate it. The ask felt impossible. But deep down, we knew God was telling us to do it.

Stepping out on faith meant saying yes to a journey without a clear ending, only a deep conviction that God wanted us to create a place for these children. We had no money to start, but we stepped out anyway. And as we trusted God with our "yes," He provided—piece by piece, miracle by miracle.

The Miracles Begin

One miracle came through a chance encounter at an airport in Amsterdam. Pastor Gary Hart had brought a team from his church, Victory Church, in Great Falls, Montana, to install playground equipment for the orphanage. The equipment had to be shipped in from

Germany. The W. A. Devore family provided it in honor of their son, Jason. After the week of labor, the Montana team was returning through Amsterdam on their way home.

A man overheard them talking about the orphanage in Ukraine. He approached Pastor Gary and began questioning him about their activity in Ukraine. He said, *"I'd like to help orphans in Ukraine,"* so Gary gave him my number. A few days later, he called our office. He introduced himself and told me how he met the Montana team and got my number. As we talked, he told me he was going to Ukraine. So, I suggested he take whatever money he wanted to contribute to help orphans with him, assuring him he would find plenty of opportunities to help children in need. He said, *"If I sent it to you, would you promise it would all go to help orphans?"* I replied, *"Of course."*

I'd never met him, so I did not anticipate it going further. A few days later, I received $5,000 in the mail from him, a perfect stranger. A few days after that, we received a phone call from his girlfriend in New Zealand, entirely out of the blue. She said, *"I can't let him beat me in this. Can I also send you $5,000 for the orphanage?"* Obviously, we were beginning to see that God was moving.

After the girlfriend called, he called again and told me he was a financial adviser with a mailing list. He asked me if I cared that he told his clients about the orphanage project in his newsletter. After this, we received checks from various states from people we had never heard of, some for $100, others for $200, and more. House of Joy orphanage was well on its way to being established.

Every step of obedience brought another provision, and our faith grew stronger each time.

But it wasn't just financial miracles. Countless times we saw God orchestrate things far beyond our control. The building was old and needed massive renovations. One of the biggest challenges was the heating system. We installed a state-of-the-art system that was supposed to provide heat for the entire complex, including the kindergarten attached to the orphanage. It was a considerable investment, and we were proud of the work we had done. But as soon as winter arrived, I received a phone call: *"The heat isn't working."*

CHALLENGES AND GOD'S TIMING

I was back in the States at the time and couldn't believe what I heard. After all that work, how could the heating system fail? They told me the system couldn't function properly because the city didn't have a gas line large enough to supply the energy we needed for such a facility. The solution? We would need to install a new gas line for that part of the city—a project estimated to cost between $60,000 and $80,000. And we were running out of money.

I was angry and frustrated. Why hadn't anyone told us this earlier? We had invested everything into this project, and now the children were freezing in the winter. But even in the midst of my frustration, God was still at work. Ukraine experienced one of the warmest winters on record that year. The staff managed to get by with space heaters, and though it was far from ideal, God provided enough warmth to get us through that season.

DIVINE PROVISION

By spring, I was invited to speak at a church in the States. The pastor asked me to briefly share about the orphanage in the evening service. I didn't think much of it. There were maybe a couple hundred people present—and I wasn't expecting any significant outcome from sharing our story. I mentioned the heating problem, and that was that.

After the service, we went to a local restaurant. As we were leaving, a man from the church called my name across the parking lot. He had been in the service and wanted to know more about the heating issue. *"What's it going to take to fix it?"* he asked. I explained the situation, and he nodded. *"Okay,"* he said and walked away.

A week later, I received a handwritten note from him. It said, *"I don't usually do things like this, but I can't get away from it. Hope you get everything you need for your heat."* Inside was a check for $100,000. God had moved in his heart to give us exactly what we needed. I still have that note as a reminder of the man's generosity and a testament to God's faithfulness. When you step out on faith, God provides. He doesn't always provide immediately or in the way you expect, but He *always* comes through.

TRUSTING GOD'S GUIDANCE OVER HUMAN LOGIC

One of the most complex parts of this journey was learning to trust God's direction, even when it didn't make sense. Initially, I planned to have an American couple we knew run the orphanage. They were childless and wanted to move to Ukraine. It seemed like the logical choice. But as we moved forward, it didn't feel right. Something was off in my spirit. I've learned to wait when I have that internal troubled feeling with no peace. God's peace is a great guide. Colossians 3:15 says, *"Let the peace of Christ rule in your hearts."* The word "rule" means "umpire."

I kept sensing that a Ukrainian woman named Lubov was the right person to lead the orphanage. Her name Lubov means love. She was the head of the education department in Kakhovka and the one who initially approached us about the project. This made no sense to me in my natural human logic—she didn't seem particularly strong in her faith and was already deeply involved in the government. But I couldn't shake the feeling that God was directing us to put her in charge.

Reluctantly, I trusted God's guidance. We made her the director, and what happened next was beyond anything I could have anticipated. Over time, Lubov became a spiritual leader for the children in the orphanage. She talked to them about God and taught them about the fear of the Lord. She allowed us to have summer Bible camps and encouraged the kids to live for Jesus. We planted a new church in the city, and the pastor's wife became the Bible teacher at House of Joy. God knew what was in Lubov's heart even when I didn't.

Looking back, I realize that my human logic was getting in the way of God's bigger plan. God was searching my heart, leading me beyond what I could see. He was calling me to trust His Spirit more than my own understanding.

FAITH IN ACTION

Faith isn't passive. It's not just a feeling; it's an action. In every one of the miracles recorded in John's Gospel, the beneficiaries of God's goodness had to act in belief. Whether it was the nobleman whose son was healed (John 4:46-54) or the man who had been infirm for thirty-eight years (John 5:1-9), faith required movement.

For Pam and me, our journey in Ukraine was a continual choice to act in belief. There were so many moments when it would have been easier to give up—to walk away from the challenges and frustrations. But each time, God reminded us that stepping out on nothing and landing on something meant trusting Him through the entire process. It meant believing that even when we couldn't see the whole picture, He was still in control.

LANDING ON SOMETHING: A LEGACY OF FAITH

For years, House of Joy has stood as a testament to God's faithfulness for us. It was more than just a building; it was a place where children could find hope, love, and the transforming power of Jesus. Looking back, I realize that every step of obedience was worth it. We didn't always know where the subsequent provision would come from, but God always provided.

Even our children, Drew and Natalie, say moving to Ukraine was one of our best decisions. The very thing I dreaded—the uncertainty, the discomfort—became one of the greatest blessings in our lives. I often reflect on the words that God spoke to me at the altar during the meeting in Oklahoma City, *"If you do this, I will bless you."* Psalm 37:5 says, *"Commit your way to the Lord; trust in him and he will do this."*

Faith is stepping out on nothing and landing on something. It's trusting that when God calls you, He will provide the way. When we look at the stories of miracles in the Bible, they all have one thing in common: People had to act in belief. Faith isn't just a feeling; it's a choice to step out, even when you don't see the ground beneath you. And when you do, God will ensure that you land on something solid—His faithfulness.

God's timing is always perfect, even when it doesn't align with our plans. Faith is trusting in that timing, stepping out when He says go, and believing that you will land precisely where He wants you to be.

This chapter is not just about our journey in Ukraine; it's about the faith journey that we are all on. Whatever God is calling you to do, know that He will provide. You need to step out in faith and trust that when you do, you'll land on something far greater than you could have ever imagined.

BELIEF IS A CHOICE, BELIEF IS AN ACTION

In all these stories, including our journey with House of Joy, the underlying truth is simple: ***Belief is a choice, belief is an action***. These eight words are a powerful reminder of how faith works daily. Faith is not passive—it's alive and dynamic and calls us to move. James 2:17 says, *"In the same way, faith by itself, if it is not accompanied by action, is dead."*

When discussing ***belief*** is a ***choice***, it means we can choose to either trust God or rely on our understanding when faced with uncertainty or adversity. ***Belief*** isn't just a feeling or an emotion that comes and goes; it's a deliberate decision to say, *"I will trust in what God has promised, even though I can't see the outcome."* The nobleman in John 4 had to choose ***belief*** when he traveled miles to ask Jesus to heal his son. He had no tangible proof that Jesus would do it, but he decided to trust and take ***action***.

The second part of those eight words—*belief* is an *action*—is what takes that *choice* and puts it into motion. The Bible is filled with examples of people who *acted* on their *beliefs*. They didn't just sit around waiting for things to happen. They stepped out, often without seeing the whole picture, trusting that God would honor their faith. The man at the pool in John 5 had been waiting thirty-eight years for a miracle, but it wasn't until Jesus said, *"Rise, take up your bed and walk,"* that he was healed. He had to **act** in *belief*, as did the blind man in John 9, who had to journey to the pool to wash away the mud and spit. These stories teach us that *belief* without *action* is incomplete.

Acting in *belief* meant moving forward with the orphanage, even when our financials didn't add up. It meant trusting that God would provide despite the obstacles. When we stepped out, He met us at every turn. **Belief is a choice that requires action.** Whether it was installing a heating system we didn't know how to pay for or trusting a Ukrainian woman with the leadership of the orphanage, we had to choose to *believe* and *act* on that belief.

You see, faith doesn't mean you'll always have clarity or a road map laid out before you. But God makes a way where there seems to be no way. Reflect on those eight words: **Belief is a choice, belief is an action**. I want to encourage you to make that choice daily. Step out and take the action that your belief demands. Trust that God will meet you, just as He did with us.

The call to create House of Joy orphanage didn't come from human ambition; it was a desire placed in our hearts by God. That is the key! It was not our idea. From the beginning, we knew this orphanage wasn't just a good idea—it was a God idea. And when God places something in your heart, He also provides the means to bring it to life.

I am not talking about just dreaming up something we want. But when God plants a dream in your heart, and you know that it came from Him, you begin to take steps toward the goal He set before you. Even though the assignment may look impossible, begin to take steps in faith, trusting Him to bring it to fruition.

There were so many moments when it felt like we were stepping out on nothing, trusting that God would place something in our hands at the right moment. Whether it was the provision of $100,000 for the heating system or the miraculous way Lubov became the director, God consistently gave us what we needed to fulfill His vision.

I want you to remember that God doesn't just give you a dream or a calling without equipping you. If He places something in your heart, He will place the resources, people, and opportunities in your hand to accomplish it.

If God puts it in your heart, He will put it in your hand . . .

CHAPTER 6

IF GOD PUTS IT IN YOUR HEART, HE WILL PUT IT IN YOUR HAND

WHEN GOD PLANTS A vision or burden in your heart, He never leaves you to accomplish it alone. But the journey from the birth of that vision to its fulfillment can be filled with moments of uncertainty, questioning, and waiting. God gives us a calling, a purpose, a dream, and promises to provide everything we need to fulfill it. This provision doesn't always come immediately, nor does it look the way we expect, but it will come. **If God puts it in your heart, He will put it in your hand.** The question is, will you have the patience, faith, and perseverance to walk through the unknown until He does?

Earlier, I stated how certain I was that we would move to Ukraine. Here's the rest of that story.

While I spent that week in Stavropol, Russia, in early 1993, I had two significant encounters with the Lord. The first was hearing His voice in that school saying those three life-changing words to me: *"Kyiv, live here."* The other experience occurred three days later on a Sunday morning.

We were invited to worship at a local church in the morning, as our crusade service was in the afternoon. The church was a former underground church and had only had the privilege of meeting publicly for about two years. The believers were still very wary and cautious regarding the government. Who could blame them? This church met in a house. It was jammed to the walls with people. They ushered us to the front row to sit on a narrow slat bench. At that point, I knew virtually no Russian. I did not know what was being said, nor did I understand the words of the songs. It didn't matter. God was about to send me a message. Remember, just three days earlier, I was told to move my family to Kyiv. I am struggling with "why." Then, God showed me.

I am reluctant to share this because visions like this are not common. But the only way I can describe it is that it was an open vision. My eyes were wide open, and I began crying almost uncontrollably because I could see masses of people scrolling past me in panoramic vision. The best way I can describe what He was showing me is that the day would come when we could not as freely bring the Gospel to these spiritually starved people as we could at that time. There was a period of a few years when the door to the Gospel was flung as wide open as you could imagine. It was an opportunity that needed to be moved on quickly.

Even though all the doors that were open then are not all open now, there is still an open door. That vision still compels us forward.

THE SEED OF A VISION

Every great move of God begins with a seed—a small idea, a nudge, or a burden He places in your heart. For Pam and me, the seed of what would become House of Joy, the orphanage in Ukraine, was planted long before we ever set foot in the country. It wasn't something we had planned or even imagined doing. Yet, when the call came from the education director in Kakhovka asking us to help establish an orphanage, we both knew that God was placing this vision in our hearts. It wasn't just an opportunity; it was a divine assignment.

This wasn't the first time God planted a vision and followed it with the provision in my life. Looking back, I can see how often God placed something on my heart that seemed impossible at the time, yet He provided exactly what we needed, often in ways I could never have foreseen. But here's the key: The journey from receiving a vision to seeing it fulfilled is never straightforward.

God rarely gives us the complete picture at once. Instead, He gives us just enough light for the next step, asking us to trust Him for the rest. It is similar to driving a car at night. Your destination may be ten miles away. When your headlights come on, they do not illuminate the entire ten miles but just the next several hundred yards. As you move forward, the light continues to reveal the road you are to take. If we could see all the potholes that exist throughout the entire journey, we might be discouraged. God shows us enough that we desire to keep going. That is how faith works—it's not about having all the answers but about trusting the One who does.

THE STRUGGLE WITH OBEDIENCE AND WAITING

Obedience is the first and most crucial step in bringing God's vision to life. But obedience can be challenging, especially when it means stepping out into the unknown. Take Abraham, for example. When God told him to leave his country and go to a land He would show him, Abraham had no idea where he was going. He simply obeyed, trusting God would reveal the destination in time (Genesis 12:1-4). Abraham's faith was counted to him as righteousness because he obeyed without knowing all the details.

For Pam and me, saying yes to the orphanage project was our first act of obedience. We didn't know where the funding would come from, how we would navigate the local government, or what obstacles we might face along the way. But we knew that God had spoken, and our job was to trust and obey. However, obedience is rarely a one-time event. It's a process of continually surrendering to God's will, especially in seasons of waiting.

Waiting is perhaps the most challenging part of the faith journey. After we had committed to the orphanage, there was a period of six months when it seemed like nothing was happening. We had taken the initial step of obedience, but now we found ourselves in a holding pattern. During that time, doubt crept in. Did we really hear from God? Why wasn't anything moving forward? What were we supposed to do while we waited?

God's timing is perfect, but it rarely aligns with our expectations. Often, we feel like God is silent, but He is working behind the scenes, preparing hearts, aligning circumstances, and positioning resources. I've learned that God uses these waiting periods to refine our faith and teach us to trust Him more deeply. The journey of faith isn't just about reaching the destination; it's about growing in our relationship with God along the way.

When Provision Comes in Unexpected Ways

God's provision doesn't always come in the ways we expect. One of the greatest lessons I've learned is that while we may have our own ideas about how God will provide, His ways are higher than ours (Isaiah 55:8-9). We often want the entire plan laid out before us, but God calls us to walk by faith, not by sight (2 Corinthians 5:7).

God moved to open the door to Ukraine through unexpected means. After my experiences in Stavropol, Russia, in 1993, I told OneHope that if they ever had an opening in Ukraine, I would be interested. I did not tell them about Kyiv, just Ukraine. Later that year, they called and asked me to go to Sevastopol, Ukraine. I looked at a map. It was about as far from Kyiv in Ukraine as you could get and still be in Ukraine. In honesty, I was hoping I had not heard clearly about moving to Kyiv at that point.

A month or so before we were to leave for Sevastopol, OneHope called and said the government had closed that city because it was a military city. They said, *"But we just had a door open to Kyiv, Ukraine. Would you be willing to go and be the speaker at our crusade in Kyiv?"*

Remember, when God spoke to me to move to Ukraine, He said Kyiv specifically. As you can imagine, I didn't have to pray; I just needed to obey and go.

While we were in Kyiv, OneHope lodged our group at a hotel named the Camping Hotel. Without explaining, I have to say it was an appropriate name. Oddly, there was another meeting taking place at the same time in that hotel. Kyiv was a city of three million people. The locals had many choices of hotels in which to have meetings.

The national bishop for the Union of Pentecostal Churches had previously sent a message to all twenty-five state bishops that he wanted them to join him in Kyiv to discuss church planting. He said to them that the door had been opened for them with *perestroika* to now be active in evangelism and plant churches, exactly what God had put in my heart to move to Ukraine for. Only in God's providence did Bishop Mykola Melnyk choose the same hotel for his meetings that our team was in.

During that week, we would have a morning prayer meeting in a conference room, and then we would leave for the day. We later discovered that the bishops, along with Bishop Melnyk and his staff, would come in after we left and have their meetings in the very same conference room. Bishop Melnyk and I did not know each other, but before the week was over, he asked if I would move there and work with them to plant churches, offering to take care of all documents required to get us in the country. All of this from an influential man whom, a week earlier, I did not know. I could not have scripted that in one hundred years. To God's glory, thirty years later, we are still planting churches with them in Ukraine.

Recalling the story about needing funds for the gas line for House of Joy orphanage, back then we had found ourselves in a financial bind. We were almost out of money, and the cost was well beyond what we could afford. I remember feeling the weight of responsibility for the children living there. Then, I received a check for $100,000 from a man who had attended a service at his church where I preached. What if he had not been there? But he was, and God stirred his heart to provide exactly what we needed, just when we needed it.

That experience reminded me that many times God's provision comes through people. When God puts something in your heart, He moves the hearts of others to come alongside and help. We are not meant to walk this journey alone. God places people in our path who will support, encourage, and provide what we need to fulfill His vision, just like He did in connecting me with Bishop Melnyk in the Camping Hotel in Kyiv.

When God's Provision Looks Different

Sometimes, however, God's provision doesn't look like what we expect. There have been times in ministry when Pam and I were praying for financial provision, but instead, God provided through unexpected partnerships or new opportunities. We thought we needed one thing, but God knew what we truly needed.

In those moments, it's essential to stay open to the different ways God may be working. Don't get so focused on one specific outcome that you miss the unexpected blessings God is trying to bring into your life. Provision doesn't always come in the form we imagine, but it always comes in the form that best serves God's purpose.

THE PROVISION OF STRENGTH AND ENDURANCE

While we often think of provision in terms of finances or resources, there is another type of provision just as important: the provision of strength and endurance. Sometimes, when God places something in your heart, the most extraordinary provision He gives you is the strength to keep going when things get tough.

Sometimes, God's provision isn't about solving our problems but giving us the grace to endure them. He provides the strength to persevere, even when the road is long and hard. Colossians 1 admonishes us to pray to be "strengthened with all His glorious power so you will have all the endurance and patience you need" (v. 11 NLT).

Pam and I experienced this many times during our work in Ukraine. The challenges were sometimes overwhelming—cultural barriers, financial stress, governmental red tape—but God gave us the strength to continue each time we felt like we couldn't go on. His grace truly was sufficient. **Trust the Giver, not just the gift.**

Ultimately, the most important lesson I've learned about God's provision is that it's not just about the gifts He gives—it's about trusting the Giver. God is the source of all provision, and if He has called you to something, He will provide what you need. But more than that, He wants you to fully trust Him—not just for what He gives, but for who He is.

Sometimes, we get so caught up in the provisions—the money, the resources, the opportunities—that we forget to seek the One who provides them. But God wants us to rely on Him, to trust Him as our ultimate source. It's in this place of trust that we experience the fullness of His provision. *God's will is God's bill!*

As we continue to walk in obedience to the vision God has given us, we must never forget that *if He has placed something in our heart, He will put it in our hand*. Our job is to trust Him, take the next step, and believe He will meet us on the path.

NEVERTHELESS MOMENTS: STEPPING BEYOND HUMAN UNDERSTANDING

But what happens when the provision doesn't come in the way or the timing we expect? What do we do when we're standing at the edge, waiting for God to move, and all we hear is silence?

These are what I like to call *"nevertheless moments,"* moments when, despite the challenges and uncertainties, we choose to trust God anyway. It's the kind of moment Peter faced after a long night of fishing, catching nothing. Jesus told him to cast his net again, and though Peter could have refused, he said, *"Nevertheless at Your word I will let down the net"* (Luke 5:5 NKJV). And it was in that moment of obedience that Peter experienced the miraculous.

There's something powerful about the word "nevertheless." It represents a decision to trust God beyond human reason. It's the moment when you choose to believe God's Word, even when your circumstances suggest otherwise.

In the book of Numbers, the Israelite spies returned from scouting the Promised Land. They reported the abundance of the land but followed it with "nevertheless." *"Nevertheless the people who dwell in the land are strong"* (Numbers 13:28 NKJV). That "nevertheless" turned a positive into a negative and revealed their lack of trust in God's ability to deliver them. They had seen God's promises but couldn't trust His protection.

On the other hand, Peter's "nevertheless" in Luke 5 turned a hopeless situation into a miraculous one. Despite unsuccessful fishing all night, Peter trusted Jesus' word and cast his net again. The catch was so great this time that it nearly broke the nets.

My "nevertheless moment" was in Stavropol, Russia, when God said to move to Kyiv. I did not know how that could ever happen, but He did. He only needed obedience that stepped beyond human reasoning.

THE WAR OF SURRENDER

When you have a "nevertheless moment," it often begins with surrender. Peter started his reply with "Master" (Luke 5:5), recognizing Jesus' authority over his life and situation. He had surrendered his boat—his means of financial support—to be used for preaching the Gospel. In return, Jesus met his greatest need at that moment: fish.

Surrender is the key to obedience. You won't obey someone you haven't surrendered to. Peter's obedience opened the door to God's provision, and the same is true for us. In every "nevertheless moment," we are invited to surrender our will, reasoning, and understanding, trusting that God knows best.

THE WAR OVER HUMAN REASON

Another battle we face in our "nevertheless moments" is the war over human reason. Peter could have easily relied on his knowledge of fishing. He was, after all, a professional fisherman. Fishing was best at night, and it was already day when Jesus asked him to cast the net again. Peter could have said, *"I know more about fishing than a carpenter does,"* but instead, he trusted that *God knew where the fish were.* I hope you caught that—no pun intended—He knew where the fish were. He sees what we do not see.

In our own lives, we often lean on human reasoning when God asks us to trust Him. Jeremiah 29:11 says, *"For I know the plans I have for you," declares the Lord, "plans to prosper you and not to harm you, plans to give you hope and a future."* Human reasoning is often limited, but God's wisdom is infinite.

THE WAR OF TRUST

Ultimately, "nevertheless moments" come down to trust. When we become convinced that God wants the best for our lives, we will trust Him with our future. Trust is required because we often won't see things occur as quickly as we want or in the way we thought they would. But just like Abraham, who went out not knowing where he was going, we must trust that God is guiding us to the promise, even when we can't see it yet (Hebrews 11:8).

In every step of the journey, remember this: *If God puts it in your heart, He will put it in your hand*. When the challenges come, the waiting seems too long, and doubt creeps in, choose to have your "nevertheless moment." Trust God. Surrender. Obey. And watch Him do the miraculous.

As we navigate the journey of faith, there are moments when we stand at the crossroads of trust and uncertainty. We experience "nevertheless moments" where we must trust God despite our circumstances. But what happens when, after trusting, after waiting, and after acting in faith, God says no? It's one of the most complex realities we face as believers—when the answer isn't what we hoped for.

When God says no, it feels like a roadblock, an unexpected twist that leaves us questioning everything. In those moments, how we respond can determine the direction of our journey moving forward.

Your response to no will determine where you go. Will you become bitter and frustrated, allowing disappointment to cloud your faith, or will you trust God's wisdom and plan, even when it doesn't align with your desires?

This isn't just a matter of circumstance—it's a battle that takes place in your mind. It comes down to changing your thoughts. When God says no, it's easy to let negative thoughts creep in—thoughts of doubt, fear, and rejection. But here's the truth: You can change your world when you **change your thoughts**. By aligning your mind with God's truth and trusting that His no is part of a greater plan, you open the door to growth, transformation, and a new direction you never could have anticipated.

This is demonstrated for our benefit in Acts 16. The apostle Paul was in the middle of his second missionary journey, ministering across Asia Minor. He had other places he desired to go, but the Spirit of God kept saying no (Acts 16:6-10). One night, Paul had a vision in which a man from Macedonia was pleading with him to come there. They quickly reset their course and went to Philippi. In Philippi, a lady named Lydia was recorded as the first convert on the European continent. Additionally, the first church in Europe was planted in Philippi.

Sometimes, a closed door is just God's way of opening a better one— you just have to be willing to walk through it because **God is a God of timing** . . .

CHAPTER 7

IMPERFECT PATIENCE, PERFECT GOD

HAVE YOU EVER BEEN in a situation where everything seems to be hanging by a thread? You're at the brink of failure, only for things to fall into place at the last possible second? These are the moments that remind me of God's intricate orchestration of our lives, His hand at work behind the scenes, pulling all the strings at the right moment. You see, God is the Master Conductor. He's not just watching from a distance; He's actively involved in the timing of every event in our lives.

His timing is flawless, even though from our limited view, it often feels delayed, or worse, that He's forgotten us. I've realized that while we might feel like we're running out of time, God is never late. My father-in-law, Joe Calabrese, used to add, *"He is not early very often either."* He is not scrambling to figure out the plan—He's orchestrating everything perfectly, down to the smallest detail. This chapter is about those moments, about learning to trust the God of timing, the Great Orchestrator, even when we don't understand what He's doing.

During our lives, we are in training—so to speak—to be led by the Spirit. God continues to show us bits and pieces of the puzzle, one piece at a time. As we trust and take those steps of faith, it is like walking a path with a flashlight. You get to see the part of the lighted path He's shown you up ahead and the path He's shown you behind you. You don't know the whole outcome; you can't shine the flashlight and see miles ahead. When you're using the light for your steps, it's important to keep it pointed so you can see just enough of the path ahead of you to avoid pitfalls and dangers. It's the same with God's leading for your life. You have to be willing to take the steps He gives you day by day and leave the outcomes to God.

I'll never forget the time Pam and I were on an old Soviet airplane in Dnipro, Ukraine. You've got to understand, this wasn't one of those nice, modern planes we're used to in the West. This relic was an old, rickety Soviet airplane that had seen better days, probably back in the Cold War era. The plane was packed to the brim, and as we sat there, I could feel the weight of the passengers, the cargo, and everything else pressing down on us.

I looked out the window and saw a stand of trees at the end of the runway. We had to get above those trees before we could genuinely be airborne, but with the plane as heavy as it was, I wasn't sure we were going to make it. You could feel the fear in the cabin. I glanced across the aisle, and a Ukrainian man was sitting there, frantically making the sign of the cross as if his life depended on it. At that moment, I realized how much fear can grip a person when they feel completely out of control.

Then, from behind, a Ukrainian man leaned forward and said in my ear, *"Unfortunately, it is an old Soviet airplane."* How right he was.

As I sat there, Psalm 56:3 came to mind: *"Whenever I am afraid, I will trust in You"* (NKJV). Trust. That was the key. I trusted a Ukrainian pilot I had never met, flying an old airplane that I had no business being on. And I certainly had no business having my wife on it. But even more than that, I had to conquer fear even when everything in me wanted to scream that this was a mistake. Fear has a way of challenging our trust, doesn't it? Whether it's fear of failure, fear of the unknown, or fear of being out of control, it tests us.

The plane's engines roared as we took off, and for a moment, I didn't think we would make it. But then, slowly, we started to climb, inch by inch, until finally, we cleared those trees. It reminded me that while we might not see how we will get out of a situation, God always has it under control. He's never late, even when it feels like we're about to crash and burn. He's not early very often either.

IMPATIENCE AND LEARNING TO WAIT ON GOD

I'd love to tell you that I've always perfectly trusted God's timing, but that would be far from the truth, and my darling wife can testify to that. I've been impatient more times than I can count. I've tried to rush His timing, thinking that I knew better. In the early days of planting churches in Ukraine, I got to a point where I was ready to give up. The people weren't responding as I expected, and I was frustrated. I wanted to throw in the towel.

I remember telling Pam, after living in Kyiv for about six months, *"We're going to quit this."* We were going city to city planting churches.

I said, *"We're going to plant a church in Kyiv, and that will be the model. And if they want a church-planting model, they can see that. This is driving me crazy."* I had made up my mind. But as I lay on my bed one night, reading Mark 1:38, I was struck by Jesus' words: *"Let us go somewhere else—to the nearby villages—so I can preach there also. That is why I have come."*

It was like God hit me upside the head with a baseball bat and said, *"Jim, this isn't about your plan. This is about My plan."* I had been trying to fit God's work into my timetable and expectations, but He had a different idea.

I knew I was supposed to be there to plant churches. God had given us all of the connections to do so. But this is where human reasoning got in the way of what God was trying to do. What God said stopped me, because I heard so clearly from the Lord. And I began to ruminate on it, and here's what He showed me: *"You're trying to plant an American church in the Ukrainian culture. It's you that's the problem. Not them, you."*

I was frustrated at the time because when we think of "church planting" in the United States, we think of a building, the funding, and the people, and all the details are relatively systematic and easy, comparatively. In regions like the former Soviet Union, people had lived in daily fear about serving the Lord, which was ingrained in the very fiber of their being, and they were fearful about having a church anywhere outside of their homes. That alone in Soviet times could get you sent to Siberia or worse. We can't begin to imagine the fear that some of those precious men and *babushkas* felt even though they were now no longer under the threat of someone imprisoning them for serving Jesus. They had seen too much of that in their past, and it was still framing their expectations of the future. Many were still functioning with an underground mentality. They had to work hard to overcome all of that, and it would take some time.

So, we began to adapt and change. I needed to change my attitude and respect the people and culture God called us to serve. After that, God told me, *"Start going to smaller places."*

His plan wasn't for me to settle in Kyiv and build a model church there. No, He wanted me to keep moving; reach the smaller, less glamorous places; and trust that He knew better than I did.

One of my favorite verses in the Bible about getting direction from the Lord is Luke 1:3. Luke's Gospel is the longest Gospel of the Gospels, obviously written by Luke. He never said God told him to write this, or that an angel appeared. All he said in verse 3 was it just seemed like the right thing to do. Luke sat down and started writing because it *seemed good to him*. Because of that, we benefit from the Gospel of Luke today. Sometimes it just seems right, and there's no other standard by which you measure whether or not to do something.

At that point, we knew this was the right thing to do: Continue the work God had sent us there to do. Instead of looking at it in frustration, we saw it as an opportunity.

Think back for a moment about God's people, the Israelites, when they came out of Egyptian bondage and traveled to the Red Sea. We all know the story of how the Lord drew the Egyptian army into the Red Sea, and then they were drowned. Think of the timing of that: At the exact right moment, God released what held back the water to take care of the enemy of the Lord. His timing was perfect. He uses timing to provide opportunity. I encourage people not to give up, even if they have a situation they've prayed for and waited for a long time.

That moment of giving up my plan for God's plan was a turning point for me. It wasn't easy, but I had to surrender my plans and timeline to God. In my mind, we should have been much further along than where I thought we were. But again, that was *my timeline*. I had to trust that He knew what He was doing, even if it didn't make sense. And you know what? Looking back, I can see that His timing was perfect. He knew what those people needed, even when I didn't.

One of the most powerful examples of God's timing in my life came when we started shipping humanitarian aid to Ukraine.

DIVINE ENCOUNTERS AND UNLIKELY PARTNERSHIPS

So, here's how it happened.

In the spring of 1995, I had been feeling a persistent nudge in my spirit telling me to ship large quantities of humanitarian aid to Ukraine, but I was hesitant. I kept pushing it away, thinking, *"I don't have the resources, the connections, or the time."* But God doesn't give up so easily.

After weeks of wrestling with God about this whole humanitarian aid idea, our family returned to Tulsa for a bit of a break.

One day, I was sitting in my office (we kept the office in Tulsa open while living abroad) when the phone rang. On the other end was a man named Francis Galloway. I didn't know who Francis was, and he didn't know me either—at least not personally. But he had a story to tell.

"Jim, I've been wanting to talk to you about what you're doing in Ukraine." He explained that he was retired, living on the West Coast, and volunteering with an organization providing humanitarian relief

to third-world countries. It was an interesting connection, and I was curious to see where it was going.

Francis told me he had recently been in Tulsa to visit his mother, who was living in a housing community at Oral Roberts University. During his visit, he attended a service at Victory Church. Now, here's where it gets good—he said, *"Jim, I saw your name in the church bulletin."*

At first, that might not seem like a big deal. But here's the backstory: I was at Victory Church one day, just walking down the hall when the pastor at the time, Pastor Billy Joe Daugherty, passed by. He asked me, *"Jim, when's your next crusade in Ukraine?"* I told him it was coming up in September, and he said, *"Call Eula Mae [his secretary], will you? Tell her to put it in the bulletin. Somebody might want to go."* Billy Joe had never done this before, nor after that. But that one time, he did.

Victory Church had an eight-page bulletin. You know how it is—who reads all eight pages? But evidently, Francis Galloway did. Somewhere in the middle of that bulletin, in a little text strip, was a mention of our Ukraine crusade. It said something like, *"Join Jim and Pam King in Ukraine for a crusade this September. Call if you're interested."* And it listed our phone number.

Francis Galloway was there that Sunday. The bulletin caught his eye. He contacted the church office, got through to someone in the pastor's office, and asked about us. They gave him a good recommendation and told him to contact me directly.

So, he called me and told me all this. He said, *"Jim, I've had Ukraine on my heart for a while now, and it won't go away."* Then he dropped the bombshell: *"I have a container of hospital supplies that I feel are supposed to go to Ukraine. Actually, we have two, but we don't know anyone in Ukraine."*

He had no contacts in Ukraine. He needed help to get the supplies there. And he wanted to know if I would be interested. Remember, I had been wrestling with God about this very thing for weeks. I had been feeling led to ship humanitarian aid to Ukraine, but I kept saying, *"No, God, it's too complicated. I don't know how to do this."* And here's this guy on the phone, offering me exactly what I had been resisting! Can we take a moment to remember that God sees what's coming long before we are obedient to what He asks us to do?!

What are you hesitating about right now? Where has God asked you to step out and trust Him for something regarding your ministry, business, family, health, finances, or maybe even your dog?! You can absolutely trust that if He has asked you to do something, then He already has everything lined up for you, down to the smallest detail.

So, back to the story . . .

I didn't jump at it right away. I said, *"Well, I don't know, Francis. What's it going to cost me?"* He said, *"Nothing. We're donating it. It's free."* I pressed him a bit more, asking, *"What's the condition of the supplies? Are they expired?"* I knew enough to know that expired medical supplies wouldn't make it through customs. But Francis assured me, *"No, it's all current. It's good stuff. Worth tens, maybe hundreds of thousands of dollars."*

He gave me two forty-foot containers full of valuable, lifesaving medical supplies for free. And it wasn't just that—the US government had a contract with their organization. They would ship the supplies to Ukraine free of charge, and I would only have to cover a small dock fee.

I may not be the sharpest tool in the shed, but I know a good deal when I see one. I thought, *"Well, if God is practically dropping this in my lap, I guess I'd better take it."* So, I said, *"Okay, I'll do it."*

But it didn't stop there. A few days later, Francis called back. *"Jim,"* he said, *"I've got some good news. We've got a third container, and we're giving that to you too."* So now, I had three forty-foot containers filled with medical supplies headed to Ukraine.

As I prepared for our upcoming crusades in Ukraine that fall, I couldn't help but think, *"What in the world am I going to do with all this stuff?"* I hadn't even considered that far ahead. All I knew was that God had told me to send aid, and now it was coming.

Fast-forward to September. We were gearing up for the first of four fall crusades in Sumy, an eastern Ukraine city near the Russian border. We had a team coming from California—about twenty people—and we were set to plant a church. Everything was running smoothly. We had our program down pretty well by then, so I wasn't too worried.

We arrived in Sumy, got settled into the hotel, and the following day, we split up into teams. Each group comprised two or three Americans and an interpreter. They headed off to schools, held assemblies, handed out the *Book of Hope*, and invited the kids and their families to the crusade meetings. Everything was going according to plan.

But then, out of nowhere, we got a call from the city administration. They demanded that I come to their offices immediately. Initially, I wasn't too concerned because the officials were cordial and welcoming in most of the cities we visited. Sometimes, they even held a dinner in our honor. So, I figured it was just some routine protocol.

I couldn't have been more wrong. When I walked into that office, I felt like I had entered a Soviet-era interrogation room. A big table of angry-looking men sat there, glaring at me. Nadia, our interpreter, was with me, and they started laying into us. *"What do you think you're doing, coming into our city and conducting all this activity without a religious visa?"* they asked.

I was stunned. *"What are you talking about? I have a visa,"* I said.

But they insisted, *"You don't have a religious visa."* They said we couldn't rent the opera house for meetings or visit schools without it. They ordered me to round up my team, get on the bus, and leave the city immediately.

My head was spinning. Up to that point, we had been welcomed with open arms in every city. This was the first time I had encountered something like this. I tried to explain that we weren't breaking any laws, but they weren't having it. *"You're breaking the laws of Ukraine,"* they said. Ukraine had changed its laws regarding religious activities that summer, requiring a religious visa for anyone doing religious activity. I did not know that, but God did.

At that moment, I felt utterly helpless. What was I going to tell the twenty Californians who had traveled all the way to Ukraine to participate in this crusade? Was I going to have to send them home?

Then something incredible happened. God gave me the words to speak. As I look back on it, I am reminded of what Jesus promised in Luke 12:11-12: *"Now when they bring you to the synagogues and magistrates and authorities, do not worry about how or what you should answer, or what you should say. For the Holy Spirit will teach you in that very hour what you ought to say"* (NKJV).

I told the officials, *"I think there's been a misunderstanding. You don't fully understand our organization. We have two arms. Yes, we've come here with spiritual material to help your people, but we also have a humanitarian arm. Our organization has two arms, spiritual and humanitarian."* I didn't tell them we were growing the second arm as I spoke under, I believe, the inspiration of the Holy Spirit.

I hadn't even thought about the humanitarian arm until that moment. But God planted that thought in my head, and I ran with it. I explained, *"In the cities we visit, we don't just provide spiritual help—we also bring physical help. We're bringing in medical supplies to meet the needs of your people."*

As soon as I said that, their entire demeanor changed. These men knew how desperate their people were. Their shelves were bare. They needed medical supplies, and here I was, telling them that we could provide them.

I continued, *"We're so structured that the two arms must always work together. If you want us to leave, we will. But you won't get any of the humanitarian aid. You won't get a single aspirin."* At that time, hospitals were desperate for medical supplies. I had access to a video of children in Ukraine undergoing a tonsillectomy without any anesthetic.

The lead official's face softened. *"Mr. King, there has been a misunderstanding. Please stay. Don't leave."* He even offered to attend one of our meetings. And sure enough, he did.

We never got kicked out of Sumy or any city after that. God knew exactly what was going to happen. He knew that the laws had changed while I was back home, and He had already prepared a way for us to stay by providing humanitarian aid. God, in His perfect timing, orchestrated everything.

That's how we continued our work in Ukraine, planted churches, and met the people's spiritual and physical needs. It opened the door to establishing the House of Joy orphanage. What I had been resisting—this call to send humanitarian aid—turned out to be what saved our mission. God's timing is always perfect, and His plans are always better than ours. To God's glory, we have been able to see 217 churches planted among Russian-speaking people.

Trusting God's Timing

One of the most challenging aspects of faith is waiting. We live in a world that craves instant gratification, and I'm no different. When God calls us to wait, it often feels like a test. I'm reminded of Habakkuk 2:3: *"For the vision is yet for an appointed time; but at the end it will speak, and it will not lie. Though it tarries, wait for it; because it will surely come, it will not tarry"* (NKJV).

Looking back over my life and ministry, I can see how God has woven everything together in ways I never imagined. I've often tried to talk God out of His plans, thinking I knew better. But time and time again, He has proven that His ways are higher and better than mine.

The challenge for each of us is to submit our plans to Him and to trust that He is orchestrating every moment for our good and His glory. We may not always understand the why behind His timing, but we can rest in the knowledge that He is the Great Orchestrator, and His timing is perfect.

THE GOD OF PERFECT TIMING

As you read this, I want to encourage you to trust God's timing in your life. Whether you're waiting for a breakthrough, a miracle, or simply direction, know that God is orchestrating every detail. He is never late, and He never makes mistakes. Trust Him to guide your steps, even when you can't see the whole picture.

Through all the unexpected turns and divine orchestration, I've learned that God's timing is not just for the big moments but for every aspect of our lives. It's easy to trust Him when everything falls into place, but the real test of faith is when things seem uncertain or delayed. In those moments, God teaches us to surrender our plans and trust His. He's inviting us to lay down our need for control and rest in the knowledge that His ways are higher and His timing is perfect. When we look beyond the immediate circumstances and fix our eyes on His greater purpose, we can find peace, even in the waiting.

But trusting God's timing doesn't mean we sit back passively. It's an active faith that requires us to keep hope alive, even when we can't see the complete picture. Hope is the anchor that holds us steady when the winds of uncertainty blow. It reminds us that God is working all things together for good, even when it feels like nothing is happening. The key to applying this in our daily lives is staying rooted in His promises, knowing that the delays are not denials but instead are part of the process that prepares us for what's ahead.

In the next chapter, we'll explore how to keep hope alive, especially when life feels like it's at a standstill, because it's that hope that fuels our faith for what's to come.

CHAPTER 8

WHEN HOPE WHISPERS: HEARING GOD IN THE SILENCE

THE WORD *HOPE* CARRIES a weight and strength only God can provide. Hope is not a fleeting feeling; it's the very anchor that keeps us grounded when life's storms rage around us. This hope we have in Christ isn't a wishful desire—it's a firm, reliable expectation that God will fulfill His promises. Hebrews 6:19 reminds us that our hope in Jesus is a sure and unshakable anchor. Just as an anchor holds a ship steady against strong currents, our hope in Christ grounds us and keeps us from being tossed about by fear or doubt.

Our hope in Christ is not passive; it calls us to persevere, to press forward even when we feel weary. The Bible is filled with reminders that our hope fuels perseverance. Romans 5:3-5 says, *"Not only so, but we also glory in our sufferings, because we know that suffering produces perseverance; perseverance, character; and character, hope. And hope does not put us to shame, because God's love has been poured out into our hearts through the Holy Spirit.*" This refining process—where trials build character and deepen hope—ensures our faith isn't easily shaken. Through each test, our hope becomes resilient and enduring.

Reflecting on my own experiences, I remember times on the mission field when perseverance was the only option. There have been seasons when ministry felt like a series of uphill battles. Resources were tight, and challenges kept arising. It's like wading through chest-high water, where the resistance slows your progress and makes even the most minor movements feel overwhelming. Yet, each time I felt the weight of discouragement, God would remind me of His promises. Persevering in hope doesn't mean ignoring difficulties; it means choosing to see beyond them, believing that God will bring growth and purpose from every hardship.

Our hope is rooted in God's character and His unchanging promises. Romans 15:13 directly speaks to this: "*May the God of hope fill you with all joy and peace as you trust in him, so that you may overflow with hope by the power of the Holy Spirit.*" God Himself is the source of our hope, and He fills us with His joy and peace as we lean on Him. This hope doesn't originate in us; it is God-given, sustained by His Spirit, and reinforced with His peace.

HOPE THAT OVERCOMES TRIALS

An essential aspect of hope is the belief that God's character never changes, even when our circumstances do. Malachi 3:6 reminds us, "*I the Lord do not change."* This truth is the foundation of our hope. While our lives and situations may shift, God's love, mercy, and faithfulness are steadfast. Hebrews 13:8 echoes this by saying, *"Jesus Christ is the same yesterday and today and forever."* We can have confidence in Him, knowing that the same God who was faithful in the past will continue to be faithful in the future.

In ministry, I've learned the power of this truth. During days when nothing seemed to go right and the work felt overwhelming, I found peace knowing that God's love and purpose for me had not changed. The knowledge that God is constant allowed me to rest, even when everything else felt unsteady. *Hope is a choice*, a choice to focus on the unchanging nature of God rather than the shifting nature of our circumstances. Desperation is underrated in God's kingdom. It means you are dependent on God.

Something miraculous happened one day in a little village in Ukraine. We were in the city of Pereyaslav conducting a crusade and distributing the *Book of Hope* in schools. It was the last day. One of the local pastors we were working with said he knew of a little village several miles away that would love to have Americans visit their school. On this team was a man named David Webb. He had been with us to Ukraine more than once before that. David quickly spoke up and said he would be glad to go. We loaded a taxi's trunk full of books. David, his friend Bob, and one of our interpreters jumped in. As they left, David asked the pastor to call the school and tell them the group was coming, as it was an unplanned visit. The pastor replied he couldn't because the school did not have a phone. He said, *"Just go. They will be happy to see you."*

When David returned, he said it was just the opposite. They arrived to see an unhappy-looking female principal standing on the steps. David was a very outgoing man. He approached her with kindness and joy. She did not reciprocate. Our teams always had gifts for the principals and their assistants. David began unloading gifts in an effort to win her favor. Eventually, she invited them to her office but did not invite them to stay. This is unusual in Ukrainian culture as they are a very gracious and kind people.

Realizing their mission of getting the Gospel to the students was going to be a failure, David and Bob prepared to leave. They had little hope. He thanked her for the visit and said, *"Before we leave, I have one more gift I would like to leave you."* He reached into the bag that had contained the gifts and pulled out two soccer balls. David said, *"We would like to leave these for your children."* She stared at him, and tears began to form in her eyes. She said, *"Mr. Webb, I have not been very kind to you."* David later said that was an understatement. She went on to say, *"The reason why is that I am a complete atheist. Do you not think I know why you are here? Do you not think educators in the country talk? Do you not think I know what you have in that trunk? I do not want these kids to have those Bibles. I am a complete atheist."*

She went on to say, *"There is something else you do not know. Our school has not received any funding this year. Our teachers have not been paid. They keep coming to work anyway because they love our children. You also do not know that just a couple of days ago, I stood here at this window."* David said from the window, you could see an old, rundown playground that was very uninviting. The principal continued, *"Even though I am a complete atheist, a couple of days ago, I stood here at this window and said, 'God, if you exist, I would just like my children to have a soccer ball to kick at recess.' Now a couple of days later, two men from halfway around the world walk in, not with one soccer ball but two. Go get your Bibles and give them to every child who wants one."*

Hope becomes real in the testing. Trials have a way of refining our faith and showing us just how powerful God's hope is. James 1:2-3 says, *"Consider it pure joy, my brothers and sisters, whenever you face trials of many kinds, because you know that the testing of your faith produces perseverance."* Perseverance strengthens our character and renews our trust in God.

One of the most significant examples of hope in the Bible is found in Abraham's life. Abraham's hope wasn't based on his circumstances or what seemed possible. He hoped because he trusted God's promise.

Abraham's life stands as a remarkable testament to the power of hope rooted in faith. God gave Abraham a promise that would have seemed impossible: that he would be the father of many nations. At the time, he and Sarah were far beyond the years of childbearing, and there was no logical reason for them to expect a child. But despite the improbability, Abraham held fast to God's word. Romans 4:18, 20-21 describes his hope in a way that resonates deeply with anyone facing the impossible: *"Against all hope, Abraham in hope believed and so became the father of many nations, just as it had been said to him . . . He did not waver through unbelief regarding the promise of God, but was strengthened in his faith and gave glory to God, being fully persuaded that God had power to do what he had promised."*

Abraham's hope wasn't blind optimism; it was grounded in the character of the One who made the promise. He firmly believed that

God could bring life out of what looked lifeless. Hope anchored in God's promises is like a tree deeply rooted in fertile soil—it may sway in the storm, but it cannot be uprooted because its foundation is secure. It's reinforced by the knowledge that if God said it, He would do it. Abraham's journey shows us that hope doesn't deny the reality of the situation but insists on the greater reality of God's power and faithfulness.

Imagine Abraham's quiet moments of reflection. He likely questioned how and when God's promise would come to pass. Yet rather than allowing his circumstances to dictate his response, he focused on God's reliability. Abraham's hope grew stronger as he faced each new day without a visible answer but with an unshakable trust that God was at work.

His hope was active; it didn't wait passively for the promise to unfold but glorified God in the waiting, praising Him for the promise before he saw its fulfillment.

LEARNING FROM ABRAHAM'S JOURNEY

Abraham's example is a powerful reminder that hope often requires patience and endurance. Waiting on God's timing isn't easy, especially when we see no evidence that things are changing. After my experiences in Stavropol, it was months before the door for a move to Kyiv opened. The waiting was a season to test and strengthen my faith.

Abraham's life shows us that God uses the waiting period to strengthen our faith. Hebrews 11:1 defines faith as *"confidence in what we hope for and assurance about what we do not see."* Abraham's hope was an assurance that allowed him to act in faith and to walk in obedience even when the promise seemed far off.

One of the greatest lessons from Abraham's life is that hope doesn't mean sitting idly; it means living with expectation and preparing for what God has promised, even if we can't see it yet. Abraham continued to trust, worship, and follow God, knowing that each step led him closer to the fulfillment of God's word.

Abraham's journey was marked by significant trials and moments where doubt could have easily overtaken him. Yet, he chose to trust in the character of God over the evidence of his circumstances. His hope in God's promises was so profound that he is called the father of faith. Through Abraham's story, we learn that real hope transcends what we can see and understand. It's a hope that reaches beyond human limitations and rests entirely in God's limitless power. Abraham didn't need to understand how God would fulfill His promise; he only needed to believe that God would.

Abraham's story is a powerful encouragement for those of us facing challenges or long seasons of waiting. It reminds us that hope anchored in God is a source of strength, allowing us to press forward even when the path ahead is unclear. Abraham's unwavering hope was not about the circumstances but about his deep-rooted confidence in God's goodness and faithfulness.

The Legacy of Abraham's Hope

The legacy of Abraham's hope continues to impact us today. His faith opened the way for God's covenant with His people—a promise that we, too, are part of as children of faith. Galatians 3:29 tells us, *"If you belong to Christ, then you are Abraham's seed, and heirs according to the promise."* Abraham's hope wasn't just for him; it was for every generation that would follow. His faith created a pathway for God's promises to be fulfilled in ways he never imagined.

Abraham's life illustrates the eternal impact that comes from choosing to hope in God's promises. When we, like Abraham, place our hope entirely in the Lord, we are part of something far more significant than ourselves. Our hope is not just for our benefit; it becomes a testimony for others and a means through which God's purposes can unfold in future generations. Abraham's legacy encourages us to hold on, to trust deeply, and to remember that when God makes a promise, it will come to pass.

HOPE THAT HOLDS THROUGH UNCERTAINTY

In seasons of life where answers are hard to come by, hope steadies us. Hope doesn't mean we ignore reality or pretend things aren't difficult; it means we cling to God's promises, trusting His faithfulness over our own understanding. Proverbs 3:5-6 tells us, *"Trust in the Lord with all your heart and lean not on your own understanding; in all your ways submit to him, and he will make your paths straight."* Trusting in God's wisdom, rather than our limited view, anchors us in hope.

While working in Ukraine and also in Israel (more about that later), there have been moments of intense struggle and impossible decisions. Every direction came with its own set of challenges. During those times, I had to remind myself of this simple truth: God is always present. He has never left me before, and He's not about to start now. This assurance didn't erase the hardship but gave me a foundation on which to stand.

God didn't design us to carry burdens alone. Hope grows and strengthens when we are in community. When we gather with others who share our faith, our hope is refreshed and renewed. Hebrews 10:24-25 encourages us, *"And let us consider how we may spur one another on toward love and good deeds, not giving up meeting together, as some are in the habit of doing, but encouraging one another."* Being in a community of faith provides a vital support system that keeps us strong and hopeful, especially during life's most challenging moments.

There is power in sharing our stories of hope. When we speak about God's faithfulness, we remind each other of His promises and renew our hope. I've seen the impact of sharing testimonies of God's work, both big and small, among fellow believers. We're reminded that we're not alone and that God is faithful to all seeking Him.

Hope isn't just a mindset; it's a daily practice. Philippians 4:8 tells us to focus on things that are true, noble, right, pure, lovely, and admirable—*"if anything is excellent or praiseworthy—think about such things."* When we *choose* to dwell on God's promises and His goodness, our hope is strengthened. It takes intentional focus, daily reminding ourselves of His Word and promises. Verse 9 says, *"Put it into practice."*

To apply hope means actively trusting God in every area of our lives. When fear and doubt come knocking, we respond with God's truth. It means praying with expectation, knowing that God hears us and is working all things together for good (Romans 8:28).

HOPE AS A LIGHT IN THE DARKNESS

In the deepest valleys, hope becomes a light that guides us forward. Psalm 119:105 says, *"Your word is a lamp for my feet, a light on my path."* In our modern day, it may be difficult to understand why only our feet are lit on the path because we have LED lights bright enough to light up practically a football field ahead of us. But in biblical times, a lamp for the feet was a small clay vessel, often filled with oil and fitted with a wick. It produced a flickering flame and was frequently held close to the ground to light the next step on rocky, uneven paths. Some lamps were small enough to be tied to a traveler's foot or ankle for hands-free navigation in the dark. They didn't illuminate the whole journey, but they provided just enough guidance to safely navigate the immediate terrain. Similarly, God's Word doesn't always show us the entire picture but faithfully gives us the wisdom and direction needed for each step, reminding us to walk by faith, not by sight. It creates dependence on Him, not on our resources or our works.

God's Word is a constant source of direction, illuminating the way even when the path seems uncertain. When we walk in hope, we're not just holding on to a positive outlook; we're holding on to God Himself, trusting Him to lead us through every dark place.

There have been times in my life when the future seemed hidden in a shadow. In those moments, I clung to God's Word, letting His promises be the light I needed. The four-year struggle with Pam's illness is an example. We found that hope isn't about seeing the whole journey; it's about trusting that God will provide what we need step by step. Just as He was faithful in the past, He will be faithful and steadfast in every step ahead.

Hope and prayer are deeply intertwined. When we bring our requests to God, we exercise hope, believing He hears us and cares about our needs. Philippians 4:6-7 encourages us to *"not be anxious about anything, but in every situation, by prayer and petition, with thanksgiving, present your requests to God. And the peace of God, which transcends all understanding, will guard your hearts and your minds in Christ Jesus."* Hope is actively strengthened through our prayers as we lay our burdens before the Lord and receive His peace in return.

Prayer transforms worry into worship. Instead of allowing fear or uncertainty to take root, we anchor ourselves in God's presence, trusting Him with every concern. It's in this exchange—where we hand over our fears and receive His peace—that hope thrives. This isn't always easy, but each prayer deepens our trust in God's faithfulness.

As we hold on to hope, we also learn to embrace the change God brings into our lives. Hope prepares our hearts to move forward, grow, and transform. Romans 12:2 calls us to *"be transformed by the renewing of [our] mind."* Transformation often involves stepping into the unknown and trusting God to lead us.

TRUSTING IN GOD'S TIMING AND FAITHFULNESS

As we think about trust, we must learn to trust God's timing. There is also another crucial truth I've learned over the years. As I stated previously, if God puts something in your heart, He'll put it in your hand. But here's the catch—you must trust Him to bring it about in His timing, not yours. I know I have emphasized timing a lot, but it bears repeating. We see this beautifully in the story of Mary, the mother of Jesus. In Luke 1, when the angel told her she would give birth to the Savior of the world, her immediate response was a question of how this could happen since she was a virgin: *"How will this be . . .?"* (v. 34). But her question wasn't rooted in doubt—it was curiosity. She believed the promise and simply wanted to know how God would work it out.

In contrast, Zechariah, the father of John the Baptist, also questioned the angel when he was told his wife would bear a son in her old age. But his question was one of disbelief. In Luke 1:18, Zechariah asks the angel, *"How can I be sure of this? I am an old man, and my wife is well along in years."* The result? He was struck mute because he doubted the word of the Lord.

There's a significant difference between asking God how out of curiosity and asking how out of doubt. Mary believed, and because of her faith, she saw the fulfillment of God's promise in His perfect time.

It's the same with us. It may seem impossible when God plants a vision or a desire in your heart. You may not understand *how* it will happen, but the key is to trust that it *will* happen. Jonathan conquered the Philistines not by sitting back and waiting for God to do all the work but by working with God (1 Samuel 14:45). There's a partnership between us and God in bringing about His plans. He gives us the vision; we trust Him to orchestrate the details. As Zig Ziglar once said, *"Efficiency is doing things right. Effectiveness is doing the right things."* God makes us effective when we trust His timing and take steps of faith.

WHEN GOD SAYS NO

There's another side to God's timing we don't often like to discuss: when God says no. Hearing no can be difficult, especially when it seems like everything is lining up for a breakthrough. But how we respond to God's no determines where we go next. Obedience to God isn't just about saying yes when He calls us to step out in faith; it's also about surrendering our desires when He closes a door. As I said before, *your response to no will determine where you go.*

I remember a time when we had a significant ministry project planned. Everything seemed to be falling into place—a generous businessman was ready to underwrite the project, and we had spent months developing the idea. On the outside, it looked like a go, but inside, I had an unsettled feeling in my spirit. So, I prayed. And as clearly as I've ever heard God speak, He said, *"Call it off."* It didn't make sense. Everything was ready, but I knew I had to obey.

That was one of the most difficult decisions I've ever made. I had to explain to my friends and partners that God had said to stop, even though I couldn't explain why. To this day, I don't know all the reasons behind His no, but that's the thing about faith—you don't always need to know. You just need to trust. Isaiah 1:19 says, *"If you are willing and obedient, you shall eat the good of the land"* (NKJV). Obedience is about our actions, but willingness is about our attitude.

Later, as I reflected on this, I realized that the opportunity to start the House of Joy orphanage came after this decision. Had I focused on something God did not want, I would have missed His entire plan. Oh, how very glad we are that God said no. Nothing could take the place of the joy we've experienced in loving these children all these years. Some are now married, doing well, and having their own families.

One of the most significant tests of our faith comes when we are faced with unanswered questions. I've had many unanswered questions in my life. My good friend, Pastor Mike Buie, once said, *"Part of faith is learning to live with unanswered questions."* I'll never forget the time Mike and his daughter Jordan, who was ten years old at the time, joined us on a mission trip to Ukraine. It had been her dream to go on a mission trip, and everything seemed to point to this being the right time.

But after a long all-night flight and just a few hours of sleep, Mike received a phone call that his father had passed away. He and Jordan had to take a plane back to the US within hours of arriving in Ukraine. To this day, Mike doesn't know why they had to go through that experience, but he's learned, like all of us, that faith means trusting God's timing, even when we don't understand it.

LIVING WITH TRUST

The truth is that trust is the fruit of a relationship in which you know you are loved. If you don't honestly believe God loves you, it's impossible to trust Him. But when you know deep in your soul that the Creator of the universe loves you, trust becomes a natural response. You can rest in the knowledge that He is orchestrating every detail of your life with love and care.

I want to leave you with one simple truth: God's no is like a detour sign on a journey—not meant to stop your progress but to guide you away from unseen danger and onto a better route. I referenced it before, but the apostle Paul experienced this, recorded in Acts 16 and 17. God had a better plan. It's His loving way of steering us toward something greater, ensuring that when the yes comes, it will be perfectly timed and precisely what we need. Trust Him in the process, even when it feels like you're in a holding pattern.

As we learn to trust God's timing, we discover a profound truth: Hope and trust prepare our hearts for transformation. Trusting Him through each season strengthens our faith, preparing us for the next steps He calls us to. And often, the path forward includes something we tend to resist—*change*.

In God's hands, change isn't just a shift in our circumstances; it's the process He uses to shape us, to bring us closer to the people He's calling us to become. In the next chapter, we'll explore how embracing change becomes a powerful way to live out our hope and trust in Him, stepping forward with confidence that every change He brings is for our good and His glory.

CHAPTER 9

TRUSTING THE CLOUD: MOVING WHEN GOD MOVES

CHANGE.

It's one of those words that stirs different reactions. Some cringe and almost consider it a curse word because they hate change. And others think it's something to be avoided at all costs. But here's the truth I want us to sit with: There can be no growth without change. Let me say that again . . . *There can be no growth without change.* You might be able to change and stay the same, but there's no way to grow without embracing the change God calls us to.

If you think your relationship with Christ is constant and has remained the same since you gave your life to Him, I challenge you to think again. That cannot be the case. When I married my wife, Pam, as much as I loved her then and as much as I knew about her and her family, it was only through the years of experiencing life together—walking, talking, and communing with one another—that I've learned that I love my wife more now. I'm closer to her now than ever before. That should be the same for us in our walk with Christ. When you have walked with the Lord consistently, your life will show noticeable changes. You will talk more like Him and love people more like Jesus.

Hebrews 7:11 informs us, *"If perfection could have been attained through the Levitical priesthood . . . why was there still need for another priest to come . . . ?"* God Himself changed the entire process of redemption by sending Jesus as our High Priest. Why? Because change was needed to fulfill His ultimate purpose. And if God—the unchanging One—is willing to bring change to move us forward, shouldn't we be open to change?

Some people think change goes against God's nature because He says, *"I the Lord do not change"* (Malachi 3:6). And it's true—God's character doesn't change. His love, mercy, holiness, and purpose remain constant. But His methods? Those can change, and they often do to meet the needs of the time. In Isaiah 43:18-19, He says, *"Forget the former things; do not dwell on the past. See, I am doing a new thing!"* God is a God of freshness and renewal, and sometimes that means we will need to let go of the way things have always been.

Here's a natural application. You probably have a mobile phone. There are over seven billion of them in use today. A friend of ours had an opportunity to get in on the ground floor years ago with a mobile phone company. He asked his dad's opinion. This was in the days when few had a mobile phone. His dad said, *"A mobile phone? I wouldn't put my money into that. It's nothing but a rich man's toy."* And he didn't. Can you imagine how much money he would have made if he had thought it through? It was not about phones but about communication. The way of communication and the frequency of communication was changing. That's all. The method was changing.

We're not discarding what's been good. Some practices and traditions have served the church well. But if we cling to the past too tightly, we risk missing what God wants to do today. Methods must change. If we had been doing enough to reach everyone, the job would be done. And yet, there are still people who need to hear the Good News. So maybe it's time to let God lead us into something new. I am using the church as an example, but it is true for the expansion of any entity.

Following God's Lead and Staying Pliable

I've found that being open to change is a constant personal challenge. It's something God has had to remind me of repeatedly, especially in ministry. The hardest part of change often lies in letting go of our expectations and allowing God to shift our plans. When I first went to Ukraine, I thought I knew what my calling looked like. But over time, as I've mentioned, God began to speak to me about humanitarian aid and meeting physical needs alongside spiritual ones. I initially resisted, telling God, *"I'm a preacher, not a doctor or social worker."* But He showed me that changing my approach would open doors for the Gospel. He also reminded me this was His mission, not mine, and I was to be pliable. We didn't change the message, but the method needed to shift to reach the people. If I had stayed stubborn, clinging to my version of the plan, I would have missed His greater purpose.

Partial obedience is still disobedience. If I had stayed rigid in my plans, I would have missed the fullness of what God had prepared. Change required me to be pliable; willing to follow wherever He led even when it looked different from what I'd planned. That's the key—to let go of our own "programs" and ask God, *"What do you want?"* God isn't calling us to add His will to our plans—He's calling us to surrender our plans entirely to Him. Staying pliable means staying close to His voice, willing to follow wherever He leads even if it looks different than we expected. As we let go of our programs and seek what God wants, He leads us into purpose and blessing beyond what we could have planned.

THREE CHANGES THAT ALIGN US WITH GOD'S PURPOSE

As God leads us through seasons of change, we must address three key areas: our thinking, expectations, and focus.

1. Change Your Thinking

Proverbs 23:7 reminds us that as a man *"thinks in his heart, so is he"* (NKJV). Our thoughts are powerful, and they shape how we live. What we believe about God and ourselves shapes our lives. When God calls us to think bigger and dream in alignment with His vision, we're challenged to leave behind small thinking and step into something expansive.

Let me give you an example. I remember being a young kid in a small church, which felt enormous to me at that time. But as I grew older and experienced different places, my view of "big" expanded. That's how God wants us to think about His kingdom. His work isn't downsizing; it's increasing. The kingdom isn't shrinking, and neither should our vision. When God calls us to "think big," He's calling us to step into a mindset worthy of His greatness. We can see things from God's perspective when we shift our thinking.

2. Change Your Expectations

Expectation is a powerful force. Isaiah 49:25 says, *"For I will contend with him who contends with you, and I will save your children"* (NKJV). That's a promise! Yet, how often do we set our expectations low, thinking God can only do so much? Expectancy is powerful and changes how we approach everything, from prayer to daily challenges. If we walk into the church expecting God to move, He will. God can do more in five minutes than we can do in fifty years.

Remember the story of my dad's cousin, Charles, whom I shared about earlier? He wanted nothing to do with God his entire life. But his mother, a woman of prayer, held on to hope for him until her last breath. And in his final days, Charles finally gave his heart to the Lord. That's the power of expecting God to work, even when it seems impossible. So, whatever you believe God for—a wayward child, healing, a breakthrough—raise your expectations because God is faithful to His promises.

3. Change Your Focus

Our focus shapes our reality. The Bible says, *"Fixing our eyes on Jesus, the pioneer and perfecter of faith"* (Hebrews 12:2). But it's easy to get distracted and let our focus drift to our struggles instead of our Savior. I humorously learned this lesson when I realized I needed reading glasses. Holding my Bible at arm's length wouldn't cut it—I had to adjust my focus to see clearly. The glasses did not change what I was looking at— they changed how I saw it. The glasses did not make the print bigger. I saw it bigger. Focusing on God instead of what we want gives us a clearer and bigger picture.

The same principle applies in life. We have to focus on the right thing. When Jesus told Peter to step out onto the water, Peter did fine as long as he kept his focus on Jesus. But the moment he looked at the waves, he began to sink. God wants us to fix our eyes on Him, not the challenges.

First Samuel 17 records the story of David killing Goliath, a giant nine feet, nine inches tall. For forty days, he had defied and belittled the Israelite army as they hid in fear. A young shepherd boy arrived to hear the soldiers saying something like, *"He is so big we can't kill him."* David showed up with nothing but a sling. He picked up five rocks and said, *"He is so big I can't miss him."* He proceeded to plant a rock between Goliath's eyes. Change your focus.

GOD'S CHANGE BRINGS GREATER THINGS

Change, when directed by God, always leads to something greater. It's never to diminish us; it's to advance us. As referenced earlier, Hebrews 7:11-12 speaks of a divine shift in the priesthood from the Levitical order to the order of Melchizedek (believed by most to be a type of Jesus). God changed the priesthood because He had something better in mind. He sent Jesus, the ultimate High Priest, who didn't just cover our sins temporarily but took them away entirely. It was a complete transformation, a better covenant.

That's what God does when He brings change into our lives. He's not taking us backward; He's moving us forward. He's not here to diminish our joy or impact but to multiply it.

God's changes bring goodness, not harm. He sees the bigger picture. Even when our flesh resists, we can trust that God has something better in mind. Again, He's taking us forward, not backward; He's bringing us closer to Him, not farther away. When God brings change, it's always for our growth and His glory. If God is calling you to change, know that it's for your good, His purpose, and the advancement of His purposes.

One of the most challenging aspects of change is letting go of control. We like to hold on to what's comfortable and predictable, but God doesn't work on our timetable, with our comfort being the only thing in mind.

A long time ago, a friend asked me to go up in his airplane with him. As we flew along, he asked me if I'd ever flown an airplane. I said no, and he asked me if I wanted to. I said, *"Well, I guess."* This airplane had a yoke, an airplane's steering wheel, that could be moved over to the passenger seat, and you could fly it from the passenger seat. So, he pulled a lever, put the yoke in front of me, and said, *"Fly it for a while."* As we flew along, he asked me how I thought I was doing. I said, *"OK."* He said, *"Well, you're doing so good, if you keep doing this good, in a while, we'll be dead."* I said, *"What are you talking about?"*

He told me that while I had control of the plane, I had been pushing on the yoke. That's because the natural feeling when flying a plane is that you're nosing up. So, if you fly by feeling alone, you will push down on the yoke. That's what I had been doing the entire time. He told me to look at the altimeter gauge, which tells your altitude. It was going counterclockwise. He said, *"You are flying us into the ground by constantly pushing on that yoke. You're trying to fly this plane by feeling, and you cannot fly it based on how it feels."* He continued, *"You have to trust your gauges."* I said, *"I don't think I want to fly anymore."* I quickly moved the yoke back over to his control. The bottom line is that we were safer when I let someone who knew what he was doing be in control. Our life journey is better when we let God be in control.

God calls us to trust His timing and ways, even when we don't understand them. Isaiah 55:8-9 reminds us, *"For my thoughts are not your thoughts, neither are your ways my ways . . . As the heavens are higher than the earth, so are my ways higher than your ways."*

There have been times in my life when I questioned God's timing and His ways. Resources were scarce, doors seemed to close, and I didn't understand why things weren't happening faster. But God was working behind the scenes, orchestrating things in His perfect timing. He calls us to release our grip on the outcome and to trust that He's already made a way. We may not see it yet, but that doesn't mean He isn't moving.

Embracing God's Call to New Levels

In every season of change, God invites us to new levels of faith and obedience. Ephesians 3:20 tells us that God *"is able to do exceedingly abundantly above all that we ask or think, according to the power that works in us"* (NKJV). When we open ourselves to God's change, we open ourselves to His power. We say, *"Lord, I trust you to do what I can't even imagine."*

As we look forward, we can expect that God's plans are greater than anything we could design ourselves. He's calling us to step out, let go of the past, and embrace the new thing He's doing. Our job isn't to know every detail of the plan; it's to be willing to say yes to whatever He asks.

He invites us into a deeper relationship with Him. He calls us to fully trust Him, lean into His wisdom, and let go of our own understanding.

The future may be uncertain to us, but it's crystal clear to God. He's calling us to move forward, not because we have all the answers, but because we trust the One who does. When we embrace change, we're stepping into a journey of faith that draws us closer to Him, strengthening and refining us.

When God leads change, we needn't fear it. Instead, we can embrace it with the confidence that He is with us every step of the way.

So, let's be people who say *yes* to God's call to change. Let's be willing to leave our comfort zones, let go of our plans, and trust that He has something better ahead. Let's lay our preferences down and submit to what He prefers. When we follow where He leads, we find purpose, growth, and a deeper faith than we ever thought possible. As we journey through change, may our eyes stay fixed on Jesus, the author and finisher of our faith, who leads us into all things good.

I don't know what changes God is calling you to make, but I do know this: He's looking to lift you up, not down, and take you forward, not backward. God's plans are always for our benefit. As we walk in step with Him, we'll find that the future He has prepared for us is filled with hope, purpose, and unimaginable blessings.

As we navigate seasons of change, we often need more than strength or courage—we need provision. When God leads us through change, He doesn't leave us without resources. Just as He calls us to take steps of faith, He also promises to supply what we need to fulfill His purpose. Even when it feels uncomfortable, the very act of stepping out in obedience is often met with God's provision in surprising and powerful ways. Provision *follows* the step of faith, not the other way around.

The greatest transition story in the Bible, beyond Jesus coming to earth, is recorded in the book of Exodus, about God's people leaving Egypt's slavery behind and moving toward His promises to them. The key to the journey is summed up in the last three verses of chapter 40. It says God led them by day with a cloud and by night with a pillar of fire. If the cloud or fire moved, they moved. If it stood still, they waited. After forty years, they had a new leader named Joshua. His first mission was to lead them across the Jordan River into the Promised Land, the land of God's provision for them. Joshua had learned they must stay close to the heart of God and His leading. In Joshua 3, we see where he had the leaders go through the camp and tell the Israelites that when they saw the Ark of the Covenant move, they must follow it. The Ark of the Covenant represented the presence and glory of God. They were saying that we must move with God. Why? The answer is in Joshua 3:4 which says, *"That you may know the way by which you must go, for **you have not passed this way before**"* (NKJV).

New territory is scary. If He is calling you to new steps of faith, stay close to Him. If He says move, then move. Although you may have not been this way before, He has. Stay close to Him. He has all the provisions you need.

In the next chapter, we'll explore how aligning with God's will opens the door to His provision. From Abraham's journey to the story of Peter casting his net at Jesus' word, we'll see that God's blessings follow when we position our lives in trust and obedience. Provision isn't simply about material resources; it's about receiving what we need to fulfill our calling and purpose and about growing in faith along the way. Let's examine how God's faithful provision meets us as we align our lives with His purposes.

CHAPTER 10

POSITIONED FOR PROVISION

ONE OF THE GREATEST lessons I've repeatedly learned is that God's provision isn't about fulfilling our every want; it's about providing exactly what we need to fulfill His purposes. When we step out in obedience and align our lives with His call, the provision we need shows up—though not always in the way we expect.

Take Abraham, for example. His journey was filled with steps of obedience that didn't make much sense to the human mind. Think about it: Leaving his home and everything familiar, he set out to an unknown destination simply because God said so. As he journeyed, God met him at each step. When he needed protection, God shielded him. When he needed direction, God led him. Ultimately, when he needed an heir, God gave him Isaac in a way that defied all natural laws.

Abraham's journey speaks to us about trust. And I've seen that same kind of trust play out in my life. When God spoke to me about going to Ukraine, I felt He was calling me to take a step that made no logical sense—to venture into a facet of ministry with nothing more than a conviction that God had spoken. I remember feeling a lot like Abraham, wondering how in the world this would work. And sure enough, just as I took that step, the provision I needed started to appear in ways I couldn't have orchestrated on my own. When we act in obedience, God meets us there.

ABRAHAM AND THE TEST OF ISAAC: PROVISION BEYOND EXPECTATION

One of the most profound aspects of Abraham's story was his willingness to trust God with Isaac, his promised son (Genesis 22). After all those years of waiting, God finally blessed him with a son. But then, in what must have been an excruciating test, God asked him to sacrifice Isaac. This is where faith and provision intersect powerfully. Abraham trusted that God would somehow still fulfill His promise, even if it meant giving up the son he loved. He would fulfill it, even though Abraham had no idea how.

I've had my own moments of testing, though none quite like Abraham's. When we were contemplating moving to Ukraine, my biggest struggle was the security of our children. That doesn't compare to what Abraham was asked to do, but nothing affects us like our children.

I have already written about some of those stories that tested my ability to trust God. Moments that looked impossible financially, like the time we were almost out of money and needed an expensive gas line to provide heat at the orphanage.

When bills are piling up, resources are low, and doors seem to be closing, our ability to trust is tested. It can be a painful and confusing time.

Now, trusting God in a situation like that is easier said than done. It helps me to go back to the time and the place God spoke to me or He placed that vision in my heart. I'm quite sure that is what Abraham did. If God calls you to this, He will see you through, just like He did when we started the House of Joy orphanage. We did not have the resources for that. He had provided the connections in Ukraine, but there was no money at the time. And sure enough, help started coming in from the most unexpected places—donations from people we did not know or hadn't spoken to in years, assistance from ministries we hadn't even reached out to. It was as if God was showing me that provision wasn't limited to what I could see or predict. He was, and is, always faithful to meet us where our faith steps out.

When you read the story of Abraham offering Isaac on an altar in Genesis 22, you realize God had the sacrificial ram working its way up the other side of the mountain all of the time Abraham was dealing with his doubts and fears. Trust God that He is working, even when it doesn't look or feel like it.

PETER'S OBEDIENCE: CASTING THE NET ONE MORE TIME

If Abraham's story teaches us about lifelong obedience, Peter's story reminds us that sometimes provision comes in single moments of faith. Remember when Peter and the disciples had been fishing all night and caught nothing (Luke 5)? I've always loved that story because I can imagine the frustration Peter must have felt. He was a seasoned fisherman, after all—he knew those waters. And yet, here was Jesus, a carpenter by trade, telling him how to fish. But Peter's response has always struck me. He said, *"Because you say so, I will let down the nets"* (v. 5).

Sometimes, faith requires us to act on God's word rather than our own understanding. I can't tell you how often I've found myself in Peter's shoes, feeling like I'd exhausted every option. There was a time in our outreach efforts when it felt like we were throwing out the net repeatedly, coming up empty every single time. I wondered if maybe we should pull back, but then I remembered Peter's story. I felt God's nudge to try one more time—to cast the net again.

Pam and I have friends from Jay, Oklahoma, named Darrel and Carol Robertson, who attend a church in a nearby small town, Southwest City, Missouri. We got to know them after their pastor at the time, Mark Short, introduced us when we were there to speak at the church. Darrel and Carol both have a remarkable life story, but Darrel has one story that reminds me of Peter's experience when the Lord told him to cast one more time.

Darrel is a businessman, rancher, and fisherman—not necessarily in that order, but he is good at all three. Sometimes, being good is not quite enough. Here's what I mean.

In 1999 their church had built a Life Center, primarily for youth. The tiny town offers little for young people to do, and the church wanted to touch their lives. It was a successful ministry. In 1999 the remaining debt on the building was around $150,000. A guest speaker on a Sunday morning said, *"I feel the Lord has given me a word about the debt of your church's Life Center. The money is already in place, and it will be paid off within a year. It will be done supernaturally."*

As Darrel tells the story, *"When I walked out of church, I felt the Lord impress on me that Carol and I were going to pay it off."* When Darrel told Carol, she thought it was crazy. *"We were basically broke."* Darrel added another twist. He said, *"I think I am going to do it fishing. I feel the Lord is going to let me win two tournaments–the FLW Forrest Wood Cup and the Ranger M1 Millennium Tournament."* Carol reminded him that, even though he was fishing in some bass tournaments, he did not even qualify to fish in those two big tournaments, so how in the world did he think that would happen?

The very next FLW tournament Darrel fished in, he placed high enough that it qualified him, if he paid the entry fees, to fish in those two large FLW tournaments God had put on his heart. Although not flush with cash, in faith, they paid the fees.

Darrel showed up to fish the FLW Forrest Wood Cup and won it. The Lord told him to give $40,000 of the winnings to the church to put on the debt and then go fish in the Ranger M1 Millennium Tournament, which was, at the time, the granddaddy of fishing tournaments.

Darrel and Carol hauled their boat to Florida—remember, there is some work we have to put into our faith. Faith is an action. This chapter is titled "Positioned for Provision." We often have to position ourselves to receive God's provision.

When they got to Florida, Darrel was hit with a severe kidney stone attack and was in the hospital the night before the tournament. Darrel was convinced that he was to fish in the tournament and would not be denied. He did.

The tournament was a four-day event. All two hundred participants fished the first two days, after which there was a cut based on fish caught, allowing only a limited number of fishermen to continue the third day. After the third day, there was another cut, with only ten fishermen allowed to fish the last day for the grand prize. Darrel battled through the kidney stone attack those first two days and made the cut for the third day. He was confident this was God's plan. Darrel needed to finish in the top ten at the end of the third day to have a chance at winning the championship. One problem. Toward the end of the third day, he had not caught enough fish to make the top ten.

Darrel said, *"I knew I needed three or four pounds of fish to make the cut. Time was about up. It was about 3:30, and at 4:00, we weighed in our top five fish. I was not catching big enough fish. I was discouraged, so I put my gear down and reminded the Lord I thought He said I would win the tournament, and I wasn't even going to make the cut for the last day and go home with little winnings."* Then God spoke to Darrel, *"Cast again."* So, he did, and boom, he caught a four-pound bass. To the nonfishermen, that is big. In the next few minutes, he caught another good one. This was enough to make the top ten, allowing him to fish for the championship.

I think you already figured out the rest of the story. The next day Darrel beat them all and won the Ranger M1 Millennium Tournament and $600,000. At that time, there had never been a tournament in history that paid that kind of money. Darrel called his pastor and said, *"Call the bank. We are paying off the Life Center."*

I know this may tempt men to say, *"I am buying a fishing boat."* If so, good luck with your wife, but that is not my point. The point? *Cast one more time! Don't quit too soon. Don't give up!*

Remember when I said at the start of Darrel's story, *"Sometimes, being good is not quite enough"*? Here's what I mean. The day after Darrel won, he got a call from Jean Short, his Sunday school teacher back in Missouri. She said, *"Darrel, what were you doing about 3:30 yesterday afternoon?"* He replied, *"Fishing in the Millennium tournament, and I had almost given up hope that I was going to win."* Jean said, *"I didn't know what was going on, but I was standing at my kitchen sink, and all of a sudden, you came on my heart so heavy I had to lay down on the floor. All I could do was pray for you."* That was about the time Darrel decided to cast again and started catching big fish. That part of Darrel's story may inspire you to pray for someone whose story is not over.

Provision in God's kingdom isn't just about money or resources. Sometimes, it's the strength to endure, the peace to keep going, or the wisdom to make the right decision. I've seen this so many times in my life and in the lives of others. For instance, my own father faced a health scare that taught our family about the kind of provision that goes beyond what you can see in a bank account.

Years ago, my father had a heart attack. He was in Minnesota at the time, and the doctors told him there was nothing they could do—no bypass, no surgery that could help. It seemed like his time was running out. But my wife, in her bold faith, called my mother and said, *"Write 'I shall not die, but live, and declare the works of the Lord' [Psalm 118:17 NKJV] on the board at the foot of his bed."* She said, *"Tell Frank, you need to get your focus on living, not on dying."*

That scripture verse became his anchor. Day in and day out, he'd look at that board and declare that verse over his life. Then, out of nowhere, the doctors found a large artery on the back side of his heart that they hadn't noticed before. Whether God miraculously put it there or not, I do not know. Suddenly, bypass surgery, which they had said was not an option, was now an option. They did the surgery, and my father went on to live for two more decades, to age eighty-seven, feeling stronger than he had in a long time. God's provision showed up in a way none of us expected—a provision of healing that brought life when we thought there was none.

Provision isn't always about what we think we need. Sometimes, God gives us exactly what's required to keep us in His purpose. For my dad, it was life and strength. For Abraham, it was a ram in the thicket. For Peter, it was a net full of fish. The common thread is that God's provision always aligns with His purpose for us.

FOCUS ON GOD'S WORD, NOT ON THE LACK

It's easy to let the lack overshadow our faith during seasons of need. But one thing I've learned is that what you focus on grows. If you fixate on the empty net, you'll miss the possibility of God filling it. I believe in the power of expectation. Every time we gather at church, we should expect God to show up. You see, expectancy is the breeding ground for miracles. When we look to God, not just for what we need but in complete confidence of who He is, we're positioned for His provision.

There's a reason Peter's story doesn't end with him catching fish. That miraculous catch was just the beginning—it led to Jesus calling him to be a fisher of men. Sometimes, God's provision comes not just to meet our current needs but to propel us into our greater calling. Peter thought he was fishing for survival, but Jesus used that moment to reveal a bigger purpose. God doesn't just meet our needs; He exceeds them to equip us for what lies ahead.

Ultimately, God's provision is a response to our trust and obedience. When we step out in faith, even when it doesn't make sense, we make room for God to work. I've seen this over and over in my life. There may be times when resources are slim and hope seems far off, but every time you choose to trust God, He will meet you there.

It has helped me immensely to have a wife who lives a life of trust and obedience. Sometimes, God's provision has come through people offering help, and other times, through an unexpected source of support. But every time, it has reminded me that God sees every need and has a way of meeting it in ways we could never plan.

Provision is about aligning our lives with God's purpose and trusting Him to take care of the rest. Just as Abraham journeyed into the unknown and Peter cast his net in faith, we, too, are invited to trust, obey, and watch God's provision unfold. It's a lesson I carry with me and one I hope to pass along—because the God who provided for Abraham, Peter, and my own family is the same God who walks with us today, ready to deliver in every season.

God's Faithful Provision in Ukraine

God's faithfulness often shows up in unexpected ways, particularly in times of crisis. I remember vividly when we were running our orphanage in Ukraine. The government had strict regulations on the number and age of children we could take in, but the need was overwhelming. Three sisters came to us—young girls whose mother was a drug addict. They'd been taken from their home and had no one left to care for them. These girls became part of our family in the orphanage, and over the years, I saw how God provided for them beyond what we could ever have imagined. I recently saw one of them, Natasha, in Kyiv. She went to college, is married to a wonderful man, and serves the Lord. Stories like hers make it all worth it.

When the war broke out in Ukraine in 2022, our orphanage faced an even more significant challenge. Russian forces quickly occupied the area, and it was clear we had to take action to protect the children. Governor Stitt from Oklahoma connected us with a company in Austria that specialized in high-level extractions in that part of the world. The team went in twice to assess the situation, but each time, they advised against moving the children; it was just too dangerous. We had to trust that God would provide another way.

In a move that I can only describe as inspired by God, we began hiding the children in private homes to protect them. For a while, we even kept up appearances at the orphanage, with staff coming in as if the children were still there, while in reality, they were safely tucked away with trusted families. Today, many of those children are in safer areas, some even as far as Kyiv, and only a few remain in their original locations due to legal constraints with their extended families.

God's provision wasn't about material resources alone—it was about safety, protection, and the courage to make difficult decisions in the face of unimaginable obstacles.

The Promise of Israel's Land: Provision for the Future

One of the most profound ways I've seen God's faithful provision is through His promises for Israel. In Genesis 15, God established a covenant with Abraham, detailing the geographical boundaries of Israel. Although the people of Israel have been exiled multiple times, God has always brought them back to the land He promised. Even though the current borders of Israel today may not match the ancient ones, God always fulfills His promises in His time.

Standing with Israel has been a critical part of our ministry. I remember a particular trip to Israel where I felt God's hand guiding us every step of the way. On one visit, we were at a military base just sixteen days before Hamas attacked it on October 7, 2023. We were allowed to pray openly on that base—a rare privilege in Israel. That was the very base that was attacked that October day. We may not know every detail of the future, but we know that God's promises are unwavering, and He will continue to provide for His people.

Provision and Promise—A Faithful God in Every Season

I've seen God's provision in action in both Ukraine and Israel. In Ukraine, God provided safety and protection for our children, even under Russian occupation. In Israel, He opened doors for ministry among Russian Jews and allowed us to help support their return to the Promised Land. The story of provision is one of patience and trust, waiting on God to fulfill His promises.

Here is how the ministry expanded into Israel. In early 1999, I was in America speaking at a church when a man approached me and said, *"The Lord told me to tell you something. What you're doing in Eastern Europe, you will do in the Middle East."* I didn't understand it then, but I filed it away. I asked the pastor, Bruce Butler, about the man because I didn't know him. His name was Joe Dockery, and he later became a very close, trusted friend. If something like that happens to you, let it be proved. Don't try to make it happen. If it is truly from the Lord, He will make it plain. At least He did for me.

Later that year, I was in Kyiv sitting in the office of one of the Ukrainian bishops we worked most closely with in church planting. Out of nowhere, he turned to me and said, *"Did I tell you we were planting a church in Israel?"* He had not. He went on to say, *"Would you meet me in Israel in December and bring your Bible school program? Something like that is needed there."* Instantly, the man in the church months before, along with the words he shared, came to my mind.

I made the first trip to Israel, and God opened one ministry door after another.

That word came to life as doors opened for ministry in Israel, allowing us to work with Russian-speaking Jews returning to the homeland. Now, nearly 20 percent of Israel's population speaks Russian, and many are Christians. God positioned us in Ukraine and Israel to be part of His unfolding plan, connecting with people who need the Gospel as they return to their ancestral land. Sometimes, provision comes as a strategic placement, positioning us exactly where He wants us.

More than twenty-five years later, we marvel at how God has orchestrated His plans for us in Israel. I don't mean just for Pam and me; I mean for each of us. He has a plan and purpose for each of our lives.

I shared the story in this book about my friend who had his own airplane and allowed me to try flying it. Remember how that went? I would have flown us into the ground because I was going by my feelings rather than the gauges. In life, God's Word is our gauge. No matter how it feels, it's not the right direction if it doesn't align with Scripture. There have been many moments in ministry where I felt like I was flying blind, but God's Word kept me grounded. Like the pilot trusting air traffic control during a storm, we must trust God's voice when we can't see the outcome.

As I close this chapter, again I'm reminded of the passage in Hebrews 7 regarding a divine shift in the priesthood. *"For the priesthood being changed, of necessity there is also a change of the law"* (v. 12 NKJV). Even the things God establishes sometimes need to change to fulfill His purpose. Changing our ministry focus to include Israel in addition to Ukraine and navigating the challenges of each was uncharted territory for me. But God was faithful at every turn, leading us and providing for us as we walked in obedience. There have been times when He asked me to let go of familiar ways and embrace the unknown, just as Abraham did.

I want to speak directly to you, the reader. If you've journeyed with me this far, you've seen that God's faithfulness isn't just a theme in stories from Scripture or the lives of people in ministry—it's a reality He offers to each of us, wherever we are, whatever we're called to. Reflect for a moment on your life, just as I've reflected on mine throughout these pages. Think back on the chapters of your story, the moments when God asked you to take a step into the unknown or to trust Him in ways that seemed impossible. Perhaps there were seasons when you felt like you were casting a net one more time, just as Peter did, unsure if anything would come of it. Or maybe, like Abraham, you've had to leave behind something familiar, taking steps of faith with only God's promise as your guide.

Now, as we look ahead, let me ask: What is God speaking to you in this season? Where is He calling you to trust, to act, to grow? Maybe it's in a relationship, a business, or a dream you've held close to your heart. God's provision and guidance are not only for the stories of old but are alive and available to you, just as they were to every person who's dared to walk with Him because *your story's not over.*

In the final chapter, we'll take a step back to examine how these principles and the promise of provision can shape your path forward. Each lesson we've explored points us back to one truth: God is both the beginning and the end, the guide through every season. As you turn the page, may you find yourself ready to listen, reflect, and walk boldly into the uncharted territory God is leading you into, confident in His faithful provision for every step.

CHAPTER 11

THEN CAME JESUS

AS WE COME TO the end of this journey together, I want to speak directly to you, heart to heart. If you've read this far, then you know by now that the purpose of this book is not only to tell stories or recount experiences, but to point you to the faithful and unchanging God who has guided me, even through the most uncertain chapters of my life. I hope these stories and lessons have resonated with you and that somewhere along these pages, you've seen glimpses of your own life, your calling, and maybe even the challenges you're facing right now.

Life is filled with unique seasons, bringing joys, struggles, and opportunities. Sometimes, it's easy to clearly see God's hand as He opens doors, provides for our needs, and brings people into our lives at the right moments. Other times, His presence feels more hidden. Maybe you've walked through seasons where you felt like Abraham, called to leave behind everything familiar and step out into the unknown. Or perhaps you've had moments like Peter, casting your net repeatedly, wondering if your efforts will ever bear fruit. Whatever season you're in, I pray that this book has shown you that God is with you in every step, eager to guide, provide, and fulfill His promises.

As a boy, I spent many Friday nights with my great-granny. I'd snuggle deep in her big goose-down feather bed and say, *"Granny, tell me a story."* She was full of them. I had my favorites, like the time she and her father, in the early 1900s, were chased through the woods by a black panther. I had heard it over and over, but I wanted to hear it again. Some stories never get old. The stories of Jesus are at the head of that list.

We humans love to hear stories. Of course, for a story to have credibility, it must be true. The apostle John told stories for twenty-one chapters in his Gospel, story after story of the wonderful works of our Lord—true stories.

John presented a fascinating thought in the last verse of the Gospel of John. He wrote this many years after the resurrection of Jesus. He lived to about age ninety. He was looking back and remembering some of the stories of the miracles of Jesus, miracles where he had a front-row seat. Yet, he said in John 21:25, *"And there are also many other things that Jesus did, which if they were written one by one, I suppose that even the world itself could not contain the books that would be written. Amen"* (NKJV).

Wow, *"the world itself could not contain the books that would be written."* I used to wrestle with that verse, thinking there was no way that it could be true, until one day, it occurred to me that it was true because the story that Jesus is writing is not over. He is still writing stories and working miracles today. I bet if we each wrote one by one the stories of what He has done in our own lives, we could probably individually fill a room with books. And guess what? *Your story's not over!* You never know what can happen when Jesus is on the scene.

As John wrote in Chapter 2, he told the story of a young bride who thought her wedding was ruined because they ran out of wine. How embarrassing . . . until Jesus turned the water into wine, the best wine.

John 5 tells us a man lay paralyzed for thirty-eight years by the Pool of Bethesda. It was a very hopeless situation . . . until Jesus arrived. After thirty-eight years of paralysis, he walked.

John 20:30-31 says, *"And truly Jesus did many other signs in the presence of His disciples, which are not written in this book; but these are written that you may believe that Jesus is the Christ, the Son of God, and that believing you may have life in His name"* (NKJV). The stories are written that we might believe today.

In John 20, the disciples had lost hope. Jesus, their hope, had just been crucified. They were hiding in fear, filled with uncertainty. John 20:19 says, *"**Then** the same day at evening* [the same day they discovered the empty tomb], *being the first day of the week, when the doors were shut where the disciples were assembled for fear of the Jews, **came Jesus** and stood in the midst, and saith unto them, Peace be unto you"* (KJV). Notice the three boldfaced words in that verse. Then came Jesus.

The stories in the Gospel of John are written so that you will believe that no matter your circumstances, Jesus will come. Jesus is still in the story-writing business. I believe with you today that Jesus will come into your circumstance just as He has done countless times in the past.

Reflect on the stories of Abraham and Peter and even my own life experiences shared in these pages. Please understand I am not equating myself with Abraham and Peter. I'm like you; I read their stories, and they give me hope and inspire my faith for God to keep writing the story of my life. Each of us has faced times of doubt, times of waiting, and times of incredible provision. Through it all, we learned to trust God, who sees the whole picture, knows every detail, and never fails to show up when we need Him most.

As I look back over the journey Pam and I have traveled, I'm constantly reminded of God's faithfulness through every season—whether it was a time of abundance or one of deep need. We've seen His hand in moments of overwhelming joy and in times of intense challenge, and each experience has only deepened our faith. God has shown us that He's not only a provider of resources but of peace, wisdom, and strength, giving us exactly what we need to continue in His plan for our lives. As you reflect on your own story, I hope you can see His hand in your life, guiding you through the mountains and valleys.

One of the most comforting truths I've learned is that God sees every need, even those we can't put into words. He knows when we're weary, when we're uncertain, and when we feel like we have nothing left to give. He comes alongside us in those moments, gently reminding us that we're not alone. I've often found that the most remarkable miracles happen not in grand displays but in the quiet assurance of His presence. Pam and I experienced this many times, whether we were ministering in Ukraine and Israel or facing other life-challenging situations where we could only trust God's provision and protection. And every time, without fail, He met us there.

God's provision often looks different than we expect. I remember times when we needed a specific resource and assumed we'd get it one way, but God provided it in a completely unexpected manner. He's so creative. He would use people we never anticipated, open doors we didn't even know existed, and bring about blessings through avenues we hadn't considered. If there's one thing I'd encourage you to do, it's to stay open to the ways God might provide. He may surprise you, showing up in ways that defy human understanding, as He did with the man who provided our medical supplies out of a simple sense of calling. Those moments are powerful reminders that God's resources are infinite, and He delights in caring for His children.

God's Faithfulness in Your Life

Take a moment to look back over your own life. Are there areas where you see God's fingerprints? Maybe a time when you faced an impossible situation, yet somehow you found the strength to go on. Or perhaps there were unexpected blessings—people who came alongside you, the financial provision that appeared just when you needed it, or a door that opened when all others had closed. These are not coincidences; they're glimpses of God's provision and faithfulness in your life.

The same God who was with Abraham in the wilderness, who filled Peter's nets, who led my family through ministry challenges in Ukraine and Israel, is the same God who walks with you. He hasn't changed, and He won't start now.

Take comfort in that truth. God is a Father who knows your needs, your fears, and your dreams. He knows the desires of your heart, and as you walk with Him, He promises to provide—not only for your material needs but also for your spiritual and emotional ones. His provision often comes in unexpected ways, through moments and people that He positions in your life at just the right time. If you look back in your own life, I'm certain you will recognize moments when God showed up on your behalf. He will do it again. Believe.

One of the key lessons I've learned over the years is to live with a sense of expectancy. This doesn't mean expecting life always to be easy or for every prayer to be answered immediately. It means keeping your heart open to what God is doing, even when it doesn't look the way you thought it would. When we live with expectancy, we're ready to receive God's provision however He chooses to bring it.

When I was facing my own times of waiting and uncertainty, I often found myself praying, *"Lord, I trust You, even when I don't understand."* In those moments, God didn't always give me answers, but He gave me peace. And as I look back now, I see that every delay, every closed door, and every unexpected twist was part of His perfect plan. I wouldn't be where I am today without those experiences, and I believe the same is true for you.

Living with expectancy means believing that God is at work, even when you can't see it. It means trusting that He has a plan for your life that is better than anything you could design on your own. It means stepping forward in faith, even when the path ahead is unclear because you know that God is faithful.

Never stop seeking Him. Sometimes, it may feel like God is hiding Himself from you. If it feels that way, it is only because He wants us to seek Him. Every parent has played hide-and-seek with their child. You hide in a spot where they have to work at finding you. But all the time, you were not far away and were going to be found. Proverbs 8:17 says, *"I love all who love me. Those who search will surely find me"* (NLT).

ALIGNING YOUR LIFE WITH GOD'S PURPOSE

One of the greatest privileges we have as believers is aligning our lives with God's purpose. When we do this, we find a deeper sense of fulfillment and peace. Our lives take on new meaning as we become part of something far greater than ourselves. But aligning with God's purpose isn't always easy. It requires surrender, trust, and a willingness to let go of our own plans in favor of His. There is power in aligning your life with God.

Throughout this book, I've shared stories of times when God called me to step into the unknown, to trust Him when the future was unclear, and to lean on Him in ways I'd never expected. Each of those experiences taught me something about God's faithfulness and His desire to use our lives for His glory. And I believe He wants to do the same in your life.

Ask yourself: Are there areas where God calls me to trust Him more deeply? Are there dreams He has placed in my heart that I've hesitated to pursue? Are there burdens He's asking me to let go of so that I can move forward with freedom? Whatever it is, I encourage you to take that step. Trust that God's plans for you are good and that He can provide for every need as you walk in obedience.

Maybe you've been reading this book and finding yourself drawn to the stories of faith, provision, and purpose, but you're not sure where you stand with God. If that's the case, let me say this: God's invitation is open to you, just as it was to me and every person who has ever sought Him. The Bible tells us that God loves you, that He sent His Son, Jesus, to die for your sins, and that He wants to have a personal relationship with you.

There's no magic formula for beginning a relationship with Jesus. It's about coming to Him with an open heart, acknowledging your need for Him, and inviting Him into your life. The journey of faith isn't always easy, but it's the most rewarding path you'll ever walk. God is ready to meet you where you are, to forgive your sins, to give you a new start, and to walk with you through every chapter of your life.

If you're ready to begin that journey, I encourage you right now to pray this simple prayer. This prayer is an expression of your heart, a way of inviting Jesus into your life and surrendering to His love and lordship, aligning yourself with God's plan for your life. If you're willing, take a moment to quiet your mind, focus your heart, and pray these words:

Heavenly Father, I come to you in the name of Jesus. Your Word says, *"Everyone who calls on the name of the Lord will be saved"* (Acts 2:21). I am calling on you. I pray and ask Jesus to come into my heart and be Lord over my life according to Romans 10:9-10: *"If you confess with your mouth the Lord Jesus and believe in your heart that God has raised Him from the dead, you will be saved. For with the heart one believes unto righteousness, and with the mouth confession is made unto salvation"* (NKJV). I do that now. I confess that Jesus is Lord, and I believe in my heart that God raised Him from the dead.

I have been born again, and I am a Christian—a child of Almighty God! I am saved! Thank you, Lord, for saving me and for giving me new life in you. Help me to grow in my faith and to walk in your purpose for my life. In Jesus' name. Amen.

If you prayed that prayer, I want to welcome you to the family of God. This is the beginning of a new chapter in your life, one filled with hope, purpose, and the assurance that your Creator profoundly loves you.

As you close this book and move forward, remember that the journey doesn't end here. God's calling is ongoing, and He has incredible plans for your life. Stay rooted in His Word, seek His presence daily, and get involved in a Bible-teaching church, surrounding yourself with a community of believers who can encourage you along the way.

My prayer for you is that you will experience the fullness of God's love and provision, that you will step into His purpose for your life with courage, and that you will be a light to others as you walk with Him. May your life be a testimony of His faithfulness, a story of His grace, and a reflection of His love. May you find joy, peace, and strength in knowing that you are never alone.

Thank you for joining me on this journey. May God bless you richly as you walk forward in faith, trusting Him to provide, guide, and fulfill every promise He has made for your life.

Don't give up. Believe. *Your story's not over!*

ABOUT THE AUTHOR

JIM KING AND HIS wife, Pam, are the founders of Awaking Hope. Through various humanitarian projects and planting churches in neglected areas, Awaking Hope has brought help and hope to the less fortunate. For over thirty years, their primary focus has been on Eastern Europe and the Middle East where they have planted 217 churches.

Forever changed by Pam's healing of an incurable disease in 1984, Jim and Pam passionately believe in the power of the Word of God and His desire to work miracles in the lives of people. The Kings reside in Tulsa, Oklahoma, and have two children, Drew and Natalie, along with six grandchildren.

In addition to their overseas ministry, Jim and Pam maintain an extensive speaking schedule in churches, conferences, and seminars. They also serve as hosts on annual Holy Land Tours to Israel.

The ministry maintains offices in Tulsa, Oklahoma, and Kyiv, Ukraine.

Author Contact

IF YOU WOULD LIKE to contact Jim King, find out more information, purchase books, or request him to speak, please contact:

Jim King
P. O. Box 700209
Tulsa, OK 74170
918-494-7772
www.awakinghope.com
info@awakinghope.com

Follow Jim King!
Facebook:
Jim King
Awaking Hope
Awaking Hope Israel

Instagram:
@jimcking
@awakinghope
@awaking.hope.israel

www.ingramcontent.com/pod-product-compliance
Lightning Source LLC
LaVergne TN
LVHW052029080426

835513LV00018B/2247